The BAFFLER

NUMBER NINE

Thomas Frank, editor-in-chief
Greg Lane, publisher
Matt Weiland, managing editor
Diamonds Mulcahey, Keith White, senior editors
Tom Vanderbilt, Maura Mahoney, Kim Phillips, associates
Jennifer Moxley, special guest poetry editor
Damon Krukowski, poetry
Emily Vogt, Brook Dooley, Emily Farmer, traffic
Matt McClintock, layout
Mark Dancey, cover

DAN BISCHOFF is the art critic for the *Newark Star-Ledger*. • ROB BOATRIGHT is soldiering in the trenches of academe. His article in this issue is somewhat related to his dissertation in political science. • For seven years BOB FITCH worked for the Communication Workers of America and the American Federation of Musicians. He is the author of *The Assassination of New York*. • Photographer DAYMON J. HARTLEY was on strike for 19 months at the *Detroit Free Press* and is now locked out. He is one of about 300 union members fired for alleged misconduct during the strike. • DOUG HENWOOD is the author of *Wall Street* and editor of *Left Business Observer*. • LYDIA MILLET is the author of *Omnivores*. • DAVID MOBERG is writing a book about labor responses to the global economy. • JENNIFER MOXLEY is co-editor of *The Impercipient Lecture Series*. • PETER RACHLEFF is a professor of history at Macalester College in St. Paul and author of *Hard-Pressed in the Heartland*. • JACQUELINE STEWART is a graduate student in English at the University of Chicago specializing in African American film and literature.

All graphs appeared previously in *Left Business Observer*, and are reprinted here courtesy of Doug Henwood. • Muriel Rukeyser's poem, "Metaphor to Action," from *Out of Silence*, 1992, Triquarterly Books, Evanston, IL © William L. Rukeyser. Reprinted with permission. • All original contents copyright © 1997 The Baffler. • Special thanks to Fantagraphics Books, who co-published this number of The Baffler.

ISSN 1059-9789; ISBN 1-888984-30-9.

Thanks to Bill Serrin, Marc Cooper, Bob Fitch, Kevin Esterling, George Hodak, Steve Duncombe, the Brecht Forum, Todd Gitlin, the Boisvert family, Kirstin Peterson, Axel and Sander Peterman, and Rebecca Bohrman. Thanks to all the alert readers who sent in material for Owen Hatteras' deviance marketing collection (he is still seeking stuff; write to him c/o the Baffler), and particularly Matthew T. Richards. This Baffler takes its particularly unhappy tone from the works of Dead Moon, Sleater Kinney, the Motards, the soundtrack to *Dutch Harbor*, and *Harlan County, U.S.A.*

Be on the lookout this fall for two Baffler books: *Commodify Your Dissent*, a selection of essays from back issues, is scheduled to be published by W. W. Norton in October, and *The Conquest of Cool*, Tom Frank's book on the advertising industry in the 1960s, will be published by the University of Chicago Press at just about the same time.

As we worked on this Baffler through the early months of 1997, it seemed obvious to us that the country was slowly coming around to the fact that lifestyle liberation wasn't all it was cracked up to be. Not only had alternative's street-cred somehow dribbled away, but even the most exalted lifestyle gurus were beginning to yawn distractedly. Take this excerpt from the *New York Times*, February 11:

"In June, pop culture addicts are going to see the definition of their favorite subject overturned when *Details* Magazine presents work, not leisure, as what defines young men today. 'When we started the magazine we thought the young man enacted his rebel pose through rock music,' said Joe Dolce, the editor. 'I started asking myself a while ago, how is a man rebelling today? Oddly enough, I came up with the idea of work.'"

See ya on the barricades, Joe!

Subscription and change-of-address correspondence should now go to a different address, where it will be opened and processed by the people at Fantagraphics: The Baffler, 7563 Lake City Way NE, Seattle WA 98115.

Submissions, letters to the editors, found objects for Owen Hatteras, and all that sort of thing should still go to the same address as ever:

The Baffler, P. O. Box 378293, Chicago, IL 60637.

When Class Disappears
Tom Frank

American liberals, even American radicals, have more in common with the Reagan right than they do with us. All of them, the whole bunch, are middle-class, Emersonian individualists. Emerson, Thoreau, all of these guys are scabs. Lane Kirkland is outside the American consensus in a way that even Abbie Hoffman never was.

— *Thomas Geoghegan,* Which Side Are You On?

Let Them Eat Pizza

IT'S a Thursday afternoon in May 1996, nearly 10 months into the Detroit newspaper strike. The city's downtown, where the offices of the *Detroit News* and *Free Press* are located, is a dead zone of boarded-up skyscrapers, vacant lots, and empty, litter-strewn streets. Down in the shadows in front of the *Detroit News* building, underneath the wall on which an inscription proclaims the paper an "Unrelenting foe of privilege and corruption," members of the six unions on strike against the newspapers are joined by union workers from across the city, assorted city councilmen, and a smattering of religious figures to sing "Solidarity Forever" and watch as this week's volunteers block the entrance to the *News*'s internal parking lot, undergo ritual removal by a squad of Detroit police, and get hauled off to jail. In the bright sunshine on the roof of the *News* building 30 feet above, professional strikebreakers from the Vance International security company look on. Were it not for their black uniforms, the thick-necked, sunglassed, and short-haired Vance guards could be actors from a beer commercial. They're certainly jolly enough: For them, the union doings appear to be rich comic spectacle. They smirk and joke. They chew gum in uncanny synchronization, their powerful jaws moving up and down in unison. And although one of them occasionally lifts a video camera to capture the moment for company lawyers, they're mainly here to provide a living tableau of public indifference.

It's not a coincidence that the most important labor struggle of the mid-Nineties is taking place in the information industry, and specifically within the smiling newspaper empires of Knight-Ridder, publisher of the *Free Press*, and Gannett, genius producer of both the *News* and *USA Today*. Labor is becoming invisible here, and the strikers know it. Most of them are Detroit lifers; many are second- and third-generation newspaper workers, with strong feelings about journalists' blue-collar social position. Talking with them below the photos of newspapermen past in the Anchor bar or at the offices of their pugnacious strike paper, the *Detroit Sunday Journal*, one begins to suspect that they might be the last of the hardened, rooted, class-conscious species of journalists that defined American literature for most of the 20th century; that the strike has, among its many other effects, served rather efficiently to weed people of exactly this type out of the journalistic workforce. Within a week after the strike began, Gannett and Knight-Ridder management had replaced them with an army of foot-loose gannettoids, interchangeable information workers who can be flown into any city on a moment's notice. While the scabs' city reporting (and, naturally, labor reporting) leaves a bit to be desired, they have had few problems cranking out the lifestyle features that draw the gaze of suburban readers. In the glazed world the info-conglomerates are building for their readers, the old newspaper workers serve about as much purpose as the buildings that once stood in the vacant lots across the street from the *News* offices. Class is disappearing from both the journalistic workplace and the public culture of this most class-conscious city.

In February 1997, the strikers made an offer to return to work un-conditionally (at press time, only a handful have been taken back) and newspapers around the country have quickly decided that the time is finally right to cover the Detroit newspaper strike. When it comes, though, their reporting is wrapped in a mythological package so uniform and so smugly confident of the direction in which civilization is heading that it reminds me of the black-clad Vance guards on the roof of the *News* building, filming and chewing. Hear the new breed of journalists confront the big questions: What is labor? Why, labor is a relic of the deluded Thirties. What are strikes? Why, strikes are sad.

The *Chicago Tribune*'s version, which appeared on page one on February 24, is positively at war with the idea of causality. It introduced its readers to the subject not by discussing the issues at stake but with a soft-focus enumeration of "the often-overlooked wounds when labor and management can't agree." There was a certain "complexity of emotions" brewing in Detroit, the *Tribune* reported, including "bitterness," "anguish," and an occasional bright patch of understanding (of strikers for scabs, naturally). The Strikes Are Sad theme permitted the *Tribune* writer all sorts of personal-relationship metaphors. "Friendships have been broken," he noted. He likened the struggle to "a troubled marriage, where both spouses have said too many

damaging things to simply forgive." He quotes a striker who says that "people have become like enemies." The article concluded with these statements of random cosmic misfortune: "It's a real tragedy," and "Why did it have to happen here?"

Since the Detroit newspaper strike was just a bit of bad luck for both sides, neither the means by which management forced its employees to the wall nor the immediate issues that precipitated the walkout back in the summer of 1995 are important enough to merit more than one sentence in the *Tribune*'s accounting. Other facts have to go unremarked altogether: For instance, that Gannett is a notoriously anti-union employer regardless of what city they're in; that newspaper management has often boasted about what the strike has allowed them to accomplish; that Detroit civic leaders, including the mayor and the archbishop, have been outspoken on the side of labor in this dispute; and that the whole thing was only made possible by one of those legislative gifts that the federal government has been showering on media conglomerates for the last 10 years (in this case the "Newspaper Preservation Act," which was interpreted in 1989 in such a manner as to permit a joint operating agreement, or federally sanctioned monopoly, between the two competing papers). So sanitized is this species of labor reporting that when the *Tribune* writer finally decided to flex his head and do some analysis, the best he was able to come up with was that favorite of indeterminacy fans everywhere, a series of "contradictions" (one of the Detroit papers was pro-labor before the strike; though the strike is supposed to be over, it really isn't), none of which are even marginally confusing to anyone who's followed the story.

The *Tribune*'s desire to deny the Detroit events' larger significance is almost palpable — and it's an especially interesting maneuver given the *Trib*'s

Photo by Daymon J. Hartley

own union-busting past. But the *Tribune* is hardly the inventor of this kind of journalism. Check out the *Reader's Digest* rendering of the Detroit story, a nasty bit of moralizing that concentrates almost exclusively on the damage strikers did to cars and windows in the happy Detroit suburb where the newspapers are printed. Even though it's openly hostile to the strikers, the *Reader's Digest* concludes its coverage by summoning up sentiments identical to those in the *Tribune* article (although here they come from the mouth of a manager, not a striker): "anguish," broken friendships, and regret over the strikers' mulish refusal to stop "living in the past." To describe labor conflicts as personal and unhappy but fund-amentally without causes that outsiders can understand is simply the way we think about the subject these days. "Unions are obsolete/Strikes are sad" is the industry standard, like "Eternal China" and the curious notion that the Balkan peoples have been at war basically forever.

The strike-as-heartbreak narrative is so meaningful to culture-industry management that it has already become a centerpiece myth in the great showplace of consensus: advertising. "Strike Break" (no kidding, that was really its title), a Pizza Hut commercial from a few years ago, presents the now-orthodox vision of organized labor so concisely and realistically that, were it not for its more-conspicuous-than-usual product placement, the ad could easily be substituted for TV news strike coverage. The scene: Anyconflict, U.S.A. Outside the plant, striking blue-collar exotics wave signs and hubbub noisily. Up in their offices, beleaguered managers, like the concerned parents of a runaway teenager, wait for the workers to come to their senses. "I thought we were friends," one executive moans. Not to worry, sir! By having a Pizza Hut delivery truck intervene with a cache of hot pies for his disgruntled employees out on the picket line, he is able to salvage the situation. Everyone knows how going on strike can build up a real hunger, right? And sure enough, the workers drop their flimsy "On Strike" signs in a rush for the pizzas, then look up gratefully to the benevolent corporate provider in the window above. Who needs negotiations, contracts, or unions themselves when friendship, the glue that *really* holds industry together, can be reaffirmed at the cost of a few pizzas?

The labor movement may be waking up from its Cold War coma, but in terms of the nation's official myths, it might just as well have gone on sleeping forever. In the millennial dreaming of the businessman's republic, labor's critique, with all its intimations about social class and workplace democracy, no longer makes sense. For contemporary American media-makers, complacent with an almost unprecedented world-historical self-assurance, the market is the only appropriate matrix for understanding human affairs. Business is life; management is government; markets are democracy; entrepreneurs are artists. And the more directly these principles are stated the better. Using a style only slightly less propagandistic than the official art of Stalinist Russia, serious journalists join with TV commercials to lead us in worship of the great executives. It is speculators, mutual-fund managers, and Federal Express, we are told, who create wealth, and the business pages teem with tales of wise blue-collar investors who have accepted the market for the universal-prosperity machine that it is and transferred their faith from union to broker. *Fast Company,* a magazine that, to the great acclaim of advertising industry pundits everywhere, has successfully merged rock 'n' roll hip with managerial efficiency, offers up a manifesto baldly equating office work with society and announces that "corporations have become the dominant institution of our times, occupying the position of the church of the Middle Ages and the nation-state of the past two centuries." *Jerry Maguire*

understands human relationships as questions of more or less honest salesmanship; French advertising executive Jean-Marie Dru writes that "people perceive countries as they do brands." Is this a great time or what?

As market-worship becomes the monotheme of official economic commentary, class disappears. Yes, individuals might suffer some species of discrimination in the workplace, but labor's more universal claims against management will not be part of the settlement. The objective facts can be recited easily enough: The *New York Times* once regularly ran meaningful labor reporting, as did business publications like *Fortune*; neither bothers today. Most daily newspapers once had writers or editors who worked the labor beat; almost none do now. As late as the 1960s, newspapers could assume that the issues and specialized language that were part of labor coverage were familiar to readers, that people knew why unions existed and what they did, that unions were a normal part of working life, and that, worst of all, readers had some personal interest in the fate of workers elsewhere. Now writers routinely address whatever labor questions they think it appropriate to raise in the specialized language of investment authorities (How will this affect the company's dividends? Its share prices?) or by passing them by altogether with the condescending usual: Unions are obsolete, strikes are sad.

You can see the consensus of forgetting even in odd places such as the *New York Times'* March 12, 1997 story on Secretary of Labor Alexis Herman, which framed her career as a Horatio Alger tale of hard work paying off but overlooked entirely her opinions on the issues facing workers. Or in the ordinarily canny Michael Lewis's bizarre declaration in a recent issue of the *New York Times Magazine* that "hostility to the market" is a form of elitism and that "only two classes of citizens" still exist that are "antimarket snob[s]": artists and aristocrats. Or in the patently bizarre explanation given by the CEO of an Ohio-based manufacturing concern for why his company had moved so many jobs to a low-wage, union-hostile Southern state: "Unionism is going down because corporations have changed their views," he told the *New York Times*. "We empower our people now." Or in *Swing* magazine's inventory of the pet causes of a dozen or so politically engaged Generation-X pop music and TV stars: Four go out for voter registration; two have made a stand for both animal rights and the environment; the homeless and freedom of speech turn the well-coiffed heads of one apiece; and the magazine even finds a star who has made that selfless commitment to "leadership training." It finds none are interested in workplace anything, even in foreign countries.

Labor unions continue to exist, of course. When one considers the millions of workers unions represent, the millions more who would like to be represented by them, and the vast millions in whose interests they act, it's easy to conclude simply that contemporary journalists are doing their jobs poorly. In fact, they're only doing them ideologically, and according to the great archetypes of our time, they're doing them correctly. Business has captured the high ground of normalcy; unions only make sense as a troublemaking special interest. The troubles and battles of working people only sound through to us as meaningless pulses from a distant universe, as personal grudge-matches between those too stupid or too resentful to get aboard the incredibly liberating and fulfilling pleasure-train of information capitalism. They inhabit, in Tom Geoghegan's accurate phrase, an

"anti-world. The black, sulfurous, White Sox anti-world. The South Side. The secret world of organized labor."

Let Them Eat Lifestyle

It's not that Americans deny the existence of social conflict. In fact, we've got our hands full these days, and with a most exciting battle: a full-on "culture war," a pitched struggle for lifestyle liberation from the dark forces of dance-floor prohibition and church-herding authoritarianism. We've got commentators who are ready to paint the entire history of the century in terms of our glorious, irresistible progress toward full enjoyment of lifestyle, with only a few brief interruptions in the unhappy Thirties and Cold War Fifties. We've got an entire academic pedagogy devoted to the notion that symbolic dissent — imagining, say, that the secret police don't want us to go to the disco, but that we're doing it anyway — is as real and as meaningful, or, better yet, *more* real and *more* meaningful than the humdrum business of organizing and movement-building. We've got a whole phalanx of cultural critics who are ready to declare victory for the lifestyle left, to describe the defeat of Bob Dole as a great victory in the war against stodginess. But most importantly, we've got an enormous segment of corporate America that has declared its "radicalism" and is busily inventing all sorts of colorful new products that will free us from mass society.

It's this last point that's most important. The culture war is a contest largely fought out between square corporate ideologues and hip corporate ideologues. According to legend, labor proved its unfriendliness to the lifestyle cause back in the Sixties and removed itself treasonably from the struggle to found irony nation. The result, 30 years later, is that our serious cultural conversation looks a lot like our daily newspaper strike coverage: Labor is just not in the picture; the culture war never leaves the confines of the free-market faith. Its more far-sighted partisans, like Richard Goldstein of the *Village Voice*, have given up the pretense altogether, correctly understanding the cozy cultural combat of recent years as little more than the victory dance of American capitalism. Where the business order goes, the culture war follows. Like the fight between Coke and Pepsi, the culture war is the American Way, extending its noisy battles over whatever local concerns are this year's target of the new global order and transforming dissent into yet another prerogative of affluence.

The tradeoff between lifestyle and labor has been so direct that it's hard to imagine that these two features of contemporary American life — one triumphant, one in total eclipse — aren't connected in some cosmic fashion. It's as though the revolutionary legacy of the Sixties somehow effaced the revolutionary legacy of the Thirties; as though workers had to be put back in their place so that rebel lifestylers could take their pleasure properly; as though urban deindustrialization had to happen so the rest of us could enjoy our authentic-proletarian conversion lofts in peace.

The culture wars have also helped to make plausible the otherwise bizarre fantasy common in contemporary management theory: that information-age capitalism has made moot what the Victorians gently called "the social question." Ad-man Dru suggests that by means of "disruption" — his dramatic term for strategic attacks on social convention — lifestyle marketers have permanently replaced the extra-corporate left altogether. For Dru audacity is more than just the quality we admire in such figures as Martin Luther King, George Bernard Shaw, and Robert Kennedy — it's the secret to brand success. Dru blithely presents a catalog of successfully disruptive brands that says more about the decline of the labor left than a dozen PBS specials about Rush Limbaugh: "The great brands of this end of the century are those that have succeeded in conveying their vision by questioning certain conventions, whether it's Apple's humanist vision, which reverses the relationship between people and machines; Benetton's libertarian vision, which overthrows communication conventions; Microsoft's progressive vision, which topples bureaucratic barriers; or Virgin's anticonformist vision, which rebels against the powers that be." The Body Shop owns compassion, Nike spirituality, Pepsi and MTV youthful rebellion. We used to have movements for change; now we have products.

Before the practice was outlawed by the Wagner Act in 1935, manufacturers commonly set up in-house pseudo-unions that made great displays of addressing workers' concerns while allowing management to avoid the costly concessions that a real union would demand. While the Republicans' best efforts have proved insufficient to revive the company union (the "Team Act," which would have done so, was vetoed by President Clinton in 1996), the principle has been successfully extended to society as a whole: We're all in the company union now, our needs for social justice served without having to go outside the system. Lifestyle capitalism comes complete with its own social justice and its own "revolution."

In the Thirties, the steel industry promulgated what it called "the Mohawk Valley Formula" to discredit and suppress organizing efforts. A PR campaign of the old school, the scheme combined a barrage of anti-union propaganda (emphasizing words like "agitators" and "law and order") with fantasies of "Citizens Committees" and loyal, prosperity-minded workers, and an overwhelming display of private

Corporate Rebels: Breaking the Shackles of Business-as-Usual

Folio:

Inflexible bureaucracy, top-down management, tightly regulated industries, monopoly – watch out. The New Economy needs new thinking, and progressive companies are turning to their in-house mavericks. These are the closet geniuses, the ones marching to their own drumbeat, the corporate rebels. Don't ignore them, or worse yet contain them, because they might just make you millions. In its May issue, *Wired* profiles eight entrepreneurs who break the rules.

"Corporate Rebels" details the accomplishments of innovators like Sherman Woo, of US West. In 1993, Woo figured that the TCP/IP technology that formed the backbone of the then nascent World Wide Web could also be used to create a proprietary online network *within* US West. He set up the first corporate intranet, through which roughly half of US West's 60,000 employees are now connected. Then there's James Howard, CEO of PrivNet, creator of Internet Fast Forward, the ad banner-blocking software that has Web advertisers fuming – and users clamoring for the URL to download it. Whether wearing suit-and-tie or ripped jeans, in their 20s or in their 40s, these eight have one thing in common: they've made a difference by challenging the status quo.

police power. Today's equivalent might be called, in honor of Nike, the Beaverton Formula: First, move your tennis-shoe manufacturing operation to the union-free and largely invisible Third World, where you can enjoy maximum "flexibility" and pay your compliant menials starvation wages courtesy of the most barbaric of all possible regimes. Second, hire the hippest of all possible advertising agencies to fetishize your products as tools of "empowerment" and "revolution" and thus make them appealing to exactly those Americans whose world has been shattered by the departure of operations like yours to the union-free South and Third World. Third (optional), build mini-museums to your seamless, self-feeding marketing vision, equating your company with human civilization generally; enjoy the plaudits of that greatest culture warrior of them all, *Advertising Age*, which recognizes you as "marketer of the year," the brand that no longer needs to speak its name.

Let Them Eat Pepper Gas

How different is all this from the days when the *Tribune* covered labor by screaming for the execution of the Haymarket defendants? We suspect it's still true, as John L. Lewis said at the start of the great organizing drive of the 1930s, that shooting people down in the streets is no longer a permissible response to union efforts. But lesser gradations of coercion are certainly still acceptable, and while calling for blood might not allow the makers of national opinion to feel as noble as they'd like, the implications of their kinder, gentler understanding of work are substantially the same as they were 100 years ago: Unions fly in the face of everything that is modern; strikes are inexplicable and tragic. The global-market ideology may gleam with the promise of new technology, but otherwise its smugness about the direction of history is as ancient as the great American fortunes. The differences between the ideologies of culture baron and robber baron lie mainly in the identity of history's guarantor: technology rather than the Great Chain of Being; chaotic excellence rather than moral order; fractals rather than human nature.

Meanwhile, the classic labor reporting of people like Mary Heaton Vorse, John Reed, Edmund Wilson, John Dos Passos, James Agee, and Ruth

McKenney seems more distant than ever. Technically excellent though we might recognize their work to be, we have trouble appreciating the infinitely less sexy culture war in which they campaigned. Classical labor reporting was beautiful modernist stuff: It sought to blend the bluntest, ugliest facts of all with the most infectious of human aspirations, to derive the transcendent from the mundane, distill the noble from the base. For today's culture warriors, the faith in the written word held by the classic labor writers must seem a little ingenuous, if not downright embarrassing. And although it is closer to us chronologically than the mow-'em-down writing of the 1880s, classic labor reporting seems to us, like unions themselves, a thing of the naive, unimaginably distant past. Books like the *U.S.A.* trilogy, *Industrial Valley,* or *The American Jitters* lack the ironic cushioning that contemporary audiences are said to demand. Nor do the republican universalism or the moral certainty of an even earlier generation of labor writers seem

possible anymore: For us the millennial phrases of Ignatius Donnelly and John Swinton or the fire-breathing second-generation abolitionism of the Populists might as well come from another planet.

But it's useful to turn the equation around, to look in these works for a key to the absences and silences that have made the culture wars of our own time so curiously weightless and consequence-free. If this nation of rebels ever comes around to actually confronting its owners, labor reporting in the classical style is something we will certainly see again. Certain assumptions of the social reporting of the Twenties, Thirties, and Forties are worth noting as both sources of the genre's meaning and tendencies forbidden by the pseudo-warring camps of the information consensus.

Classic labor writing is grounded in an acute awareness of history, of how things have got to their current state, and of how people benefit or suffer from the deeds of their ancestors. It's no coincidence that the only good writing on labor being done today is historical.

To cover a long-running strike is to encounter a similar attitude instantly. Even at a time when the market is said to have abolished history and turned us loose in a context-free universe, militant unionists are among this country's last non-academics to retain a notion of pastness, of inheritance, and of cataclysmic historical rupture. Granted, the past they celebrate is often understood romantically and sentimentally, but in the contemporary cultural climate, their insistence on memory is nothing short of radical.

While information-age orthodoxy insists that the world is becoming increasingly transparent and visible, the labor writing of the mid-20th century returns again and again to the theme of hidden history, of what Geoghegan calls a "secret world." As smugness is the narrative principle of writing about the marketplace, so a feeling of grappling with invisibility animates writing about work and social class. The facts of working life are something we have to "discover" again and again, much as Americans "discovered" poverty in the early Sixties by reading Michael Harrington's *The Other America*. Labor is the inscrutable fist thrust through the floor of the grand ballroom in the famous 19th-century cartoon; it's the hideous and literally underground land of toil described by Donnelly in *Caesar's Column*. Classic labor reporting is addressed to us almost as dispatches from a parallel universe, from a hidden America where rules of civility and democracy do not apply. Whether it's John Reed describing events at Paterson or James Agee writing about the sharecropping South, labor reporters automatically assumed that their readers would have heard nothing or only the most distorted versions of events in those places. In a time when cinematic cynicism toward the government, the military, and authority generally is at a sort of all-time high, this aspect of classic

labor writing can only become more and more appealing.

As a rule, advertising, the highest form of information-age cultural production, intentionally avoids discussing where products come from. In a time in which, we are told, style and image transcend all — both for corporate marketers and ourselves as consumers — essays like Edmund Wilson's long description of the brutal facts of automobile production in "Detroit Motors" come across as nothing short of revelation. For a writer in the 1990s to produce such a piece — insisting upon the inherently local, inherently material facts of work in an age when the only journalistic game in town is to wax blissful about how the cyber-universe is eclipsing the analog world — would be almost willfully contrary.

Most important, though, is the notion of human agency. Classic labor writing clings almost obsessively to the possibility of transformation, the feeling that the conditions that determine people's lives are things we can control. This is the feature that made the genre so powerful, and also the feature most noticeably absent from contemporary reporting on the subject. Although the ideology of the culture trust insists that these are the most democratic times of all (since there's entertainment available now for every conceivable demographic), we seem to have lost altogether the sense of democratic possibility that animates unionism. Even those who are sympathetic to the victims of downsizing (and, hey, who isn't?) understand workers as victims, not as historical actors capable of reversing the whole thing. Things that happen to us are accidental; things that happen in the economy as a whole are inevitable. Wages are stagnating even while the economy grows? Well ... the market works in mysterious ways. Economics is something we complain about; the power to change our lives is a role we reserve exclusively for business. Louis Adamic entitled his 1931 history of class conflict in the United States *Dynamite*; a contemporary treatment of the subject would be called *Tears*.

I T's a Saturday afternoon in October 1994. The workers at A. E. Staley, a corn-processing plant in Decatur, Illinois, have been locked out of their jobs for over a year by their employer, a teamwork- and theory-touting multinational conglomerate. In the course of the year they've been joined on the picket lines by strikers from Caterpillar and Bridgestone/Firestone, the town's two other major industrial employers. The global economy has dropped the bomb on this once-complacent blue-collar city. But still I had been surprised when I was told all this by a friend in Springfield; I had seen nothing about it in the Chicago newspapers besides the standard tragedy tales. The issues in Decatur are as compelling as they can possibly be: Workers at all three plants are in danger of losing the eight-hour day, the reform upon which the American labor movement was founded, and with it any hope of leading a normal life outside of work. And the situation is also maddening: Without help from above, the rank-and-file Staley workers have mounted a campaign marked by innovation, careful planning, and even genius, but their international union has made no secret about its reluctance to support them. Nor has Secretary of Labor Robert Reich raised a finger to help them win their fight. Wanting to save only their jobs, they have taken on two powerful enemies at once. Staley has locked them out and sends pepper-gas-spraying goons after them when they protest before the plant; union hierarchs, threatened by the specter of rank-and-file activism, want no more to do with them than their employer. Two years later, their struggle having ended in defeat, many of the Staley workers will accuse their international of undermining their campaign and engineering their capitulation.

But in late 1994 the battle for visibility is at its height, with billboards proclaiming Decatur a "war zone" appearing on major highways and locked-out Staley workers touring the country as "road warriors" to spread the word about their experiences. On this Saturday afternoon, 15,000 union workers from around the country have arrived for a march through Decatur in the hopes that by sheer numbers they can reclaim this city, give this struggle a prominence that is impossible to ignore.

Before heading back to Chicago, we stop for dinner at a Decatur Denny's, whose only other clientele is a gaggle of drunken Decatur high schoolers wearing whimsical hats. When the Denny's manager, an efficient fiftyish fellow in clip-on tie and name tag, hustles out to clean our table or to tell us why Denny's can't cook a hamburger rare, he is the object of some hilarity at the kids' table. They pelt his back with fries as he hurries here and there.

This is sordid, depressing stuff. But there are important qualitative differences between his predicament and that of the Staley workers. He inhabits a clean orange world free of labor struggles, union halls, and pepper-gassing by cops. But it's also a world free of history and meaning, free of the kind of the energy and friendship we had seen in the streets of Decatur that day, and, most importantly, free of the sense that the city was something you had made, that the future was a question you were answering. Do we want to be a postindustrial country? Do we want to entrust our lives to the whims of the market? Once, these were things we would have decided for ourselves; sitting alone at Denny's reading *USA Today*, they are none of our business. 🖎

THE GAUDY AND DAMNED

TOM VANDERBILT

Back in the days when I toiled for a media conglomerate, I would find in my mailbox once a month a slim magazine called *Vitality*. Festooned with time-saving tips and austere food intake regimens, *Vitality* was a lightning-rod for scorn among the staff. I often wondered what charlatanry had convinced the company to mass-mail it in the first place. More shrill and simplistic than state-issued propaganda, its main rallying point seemed to be fat; i.e., on one's person, in one's finances, at one's workplace, fat was a scourge that needed ever-vigilant trimming. If turn-of-the-century wealth implied corpulent, mutton-chopped Captains of Industry, today's slicked-down Stairmastering stock-optioneers, as well as the companies they populate, are models of slimness: "lean and mean" or "lean production"; "rightsizing" or "trimming workstaff." Out there in the all-you-can-eat fields of the Republic, girth may still hold sway, as we consume the full output of our production, but *Vitality* and a whole industry ring dissonant in the background, telling us it should not be so.

The sense of paranoia about ourselves that *Vitality* taught — our squandering of time, our poor eating habits, our drag on the organization, reflected our sense of paranoia out in society at large. "Job security must come from within," advises a recent management tract, one of many that posits a nation of self-employed people working for corporations; "only the paranoid survive," another corporate study put it. This all came back to me recently as I read *Chicken Soup for the Soul at Work*, a workplace variant of the original bestseller that is filled with inspirational stories about everyday people doing good things. The authors of *Chicken Soup* assert that there's a "tremendous malaise in the workplace today" and that with "all the downsizing, the work going off-shore . . . people need to feel inspired" — thus the Norman Vincent Peale homilies that comprise the book. One story, titled "Santa Comes to Joan," caught my eye: "Every office has a Joan, or should have. She's the one everyone looks to when the workload gets too heavy. She's the one with the good story and the ready laugh. For our Christmas party, she's the one who transforms our sterile corporate conference room, Christmas after Christmas, with tiny white lights, real teacups, teapots and plates she had brought from home."

There was a "Joan" at my media conglomerate employer, and one day during the company's year of near 20 percent profits, I came to work to find she was being let go, the result of some silent machinations from above (wherever that was). And even as the company "aggressively expanded its position" by purchasing other media entities, we would occasionally feel the brush of distant rumor telling us that our days, too, were numbered. So what was the talk around the water cooler? Plans to organize? Formal protests over the company's shoddy personnel practices? No, no, no.

We talked about *Dilbert*. Hardly a day passed in which we made no reference to that great subverter of corporate hierarchy, in which I didn't see Dilbert's winsome visage flickering on a neighboring screen saver or peering out from a mug in the employee kitchen. In the face of real threats from a ruthless and all-too-knowing management, we turned to a fantasy office world in which managers were obvious incompetents, in which new motivational schemes were self-evidently ridiculous, and in which anonymous cubicled office drones held the real power. Even downsizing seemed innocuous in *Dilbert*, a practical joke that was always happening to someone else.

What seems remarkable about all this now is the curious relationship between *Dilbert* and all the absurd management fads and mission statements that it mocks. Its refusal to do anything more than gripe helped more to naturalize the managerial culture than to subvert it. As corporate America tears up the social contract, it should come as no surprise that *Dilbert* books have become a popular gift from managers to employees, or that executives have begun to ask the comic's author to lecture at their conferences, or that *Dilbert* books have become a "business bestseller" (an entirely new category indicative of the proliferation of corporate culture commodities), or even that Hallmark should issue Dilbert mugs for "Boss Day" (the holiday invented by a Kansas woman in 1954 who says she wanted to honor her father). Symbolic acts of everyday resistance, it turns out, are healthy. They are exactly what the boss wants to see on your cubicle wall.

Like *Vitality*, *Dilbert* helps to humanize and insulate us from what is actually happening in corporate America. The two fill the same cultural need as the TV commercials that show family farmers using geosynchronous technology to plow their tracts, even though the ad's sponsor is an agribusiness concern that has made family farmers virtually extinct. Or as all the writing about homespun investment groups like the "Beardstown Ladies," whose folksy tips and "recipes" make believable the ridiculous conceit that information-age speculating is as familiar and safe as stowing bags of money under the bed, and that the global market, which uproots whole cultures and seeks to render locality obsolete, is somehow A-OK with the small-town values and personalities they symbolize.

Meanwhile, sales of less savvy and less cynical corporate ideo-products are suffering from a devastating backlash. *The New Republic* reports that the Conference Board, the folks that bring you the Consumer Confidence Index and other accouterments of the Kinko's economy, has announced a scalding assessment of the motivational industry. As it turns out, posters of mountain-climbers and rowing crews don't spur the unmotivated, and the already motivated don't need them. Even Successories, the nation's leading purveyor of corporate incentiana, has been forced to sack its management team and replace workers after a few quarters of lackluster performance.

Other dealers in positive thinking and management chicanery have been able to stay ahead of the curve. Hallmark Cards, for example, a leader in the "social expressions" category, has already supplemented its "business expressions" line with one called "Out of the Blue," a series of small, inexpensive cards bearing some quickly digestible fragment of workplace uplift. A Hallmark spokesperson informed me that the line was part of a nationwide trend toward what *Harper's Bazaar* reported as a "nicening of the workplace." The "Out of the Blue" cards, I was told, were designed to fit in employee mailboxes, or to be left discreetly on desks, somehow providing salve to the increasing tension over layoffs, outsourcing, mergers, and the rest.

Even more noxious is the "corporate soul" movement, which argues that downsizing organizations need to inject "values" into the company or bring "healing" into the workplace in forms ranging from mass bouts of therapy to flowers left on desks (as if downsizing were some affair of the heart gone awry). It was, of course, only a matter of time before the hucksters of wellness, those ubiquitous checkout-counter gurus like Deepak Chopra and James (*Celestine Prophecy*) Renfield, began tailoring their soulcraft to fit the hulking frame of corporate culture. Renfield now explains how spirituality and capitalism are compatible, observing recently that "the greatest fulfillment comes when we make the world a better place, and this connects with our deepest traditional need in capitalism — find a need and fill it." Given the increasing taste for euphemism, I suspect it may only be a short while until Fortune 500 companies follow the lead of the New Agey firms replacing their CEOs with "Keepers of Dreams and Beliefs."

The spirituality kick reaches an illogical extreme in *Jesus CEO*, a book that finds Christ's teachings applicable to today's business world. "Jesus knew his mission statement," the author observes, "and he did not deviate from it." Or, taking a metaphor from the ever-relevant world of sports (a longtime corporate-inspirational favorite), "As quarterback, Jesus knew his game plan could not be to take truth up the middle." The book essentially updates Bruce Barton's *The Man Nobody Knows*, which argued Jesus was, before anything else, a salesman. Barton's book appeared in 1925, at the tail end of several decades' effort to bring That Old Time Religion into line with the new mass consumer economy, a process that spun off such marvels as Mind Cure and spirituality-tinged bestsellers like 1907's *The Efficient Life*.

"It's like a religion," one office worker told *The New Republic* about Successories. And the comparison is entirely apt: Just as Protestant ideas of salvation in the next world were once retooled into visions of abundance in this world, so is the new impetus toward spirituality in the workplace and Scripture-like motivational tales offering assurance to those caught amid the convulsive shifts of the reengineering corporation, the corrosion of loyalty and security, and the terrifying ruptures of the globalizing economy. Religion, too, drifts toward market logic, in everything from mainstream megachurches to the most outlandish cults. Note in particular the heavily entrepreneurial Heaven's Gate, not a bunch of sandal-sporting mystics but a well-run, forward-looking organization (willing to demonstrate "teamwork" and confront "risk") flourishing in a sci-tech haven by the sea. Indeed, in the weeks after the group's "departure," I stumbled across this suggestive passage in *God Wants You to Be Rich*, a book about the "theology of economics" by libertarian economist Paul Zane Pilzer: "To survive today, the corporation must look frequently at every task as if it were about to embark on a journey to a new kind of planet on a new kind of spaceship."

In South Korea, in Russia, and in Europe (where, a Smith Barney analyst observed, "there have been decades of coddling the job holders"), the big changes of recent years have bred massive protests in the street by those whose lives are scheduled to be destroyed. Here we line the barricades with greeting cards and Fortune 500 faith-healers.

Popular Front Redux?

Chris Lehmann

The fact remains, the most civilized community is reluctant to trust its serious interests to others than men of pecuniary substance, who have proved their fitness for the direction of academic affairs by acquiring, or by otherwise being possessed of, great wealth.

— Thorstein Veblen, The Higher Learning in America

AFTER decades of baroque theorizing, the American academy seems to be working itself into a lather of solidarity with the working class. Last October, a Columbia University "teach-in" brought together celebrated left intellectuals with leaders of the new, revitalized AFL-CIO, including recently elected union president John Sweeney. More than 1,700 people thronged to the event's opening session; satellite events at campuses like the University of Wisconsin and the University of Texas at El Paso drew healthy turnouts as well. Then in December, the interdisciplinary journal *Social Text* — subject of much unwelcome press ever since it published a prank article by NYU physicist Alan Sokal purporting to refute the existence of reality — devoted most of its Winter Issue to the "Yale Dossier." This collection brought together testimonials and scholarly analyses denouncing the Ivy League school's efforts to break the fledgling teaching assistants' union, the Graduate Employees and Students Organization (GESO), and Locals 34 and 35 of the Hotel Employees and Restaurant Employees International Union (HERE), which represent Yale's cafeteria and maintenance staffs.

It seems a thaw is under way in the long cold war that sundered organized labor and the American university during the fabled upheavals of the 1960s. And it would be churlish indeed to deny that this turn represents a welcome shift in the intellectual climate. Supporting the labor struggles of clerical workers, maintenance staff, and teaching assistants is a far better use of institutional time, after all, than writing another tortured defense of the wartime activities (and postwar lies) of Nazi collaborator/literary theorist Paul de Man.

Yet there is also cause to question the sudden round of labor-academic nuptials. Neither the labor movement nor the intellectual class is as hale or self-confident as it was during the flush days of Popular Front radicalism, when workers and intellectuals came together under the banner of Communism as "Twentieth Century Americanism." And more to the point, the nature of intellectual labor has changed dramatically since the time when partisans of the Popular Front referred to themselves as "brain workers" and the notion of "organic intellectuals" had real-life resonance instead of merely theoretical cachet.

In other words, the sometimes unwieldy rank and file of Popular Front intellectuals — novelists, religious thinkers, journalists, screenwriters, musicians, etc. — has vanished from the historical stage. American intellectual life has become stolidly professionalized. The idea of a "brain worker" who doesn't brandish a *curriculum vitae* and a fistful of monographs is analogous to, say, the entrepreneurial gangster: strictly a period piece. Likewise, the institutions that harbor professional intellectuals have fewer and fewer resources to bring to bear on the struggles of working Americans for self-determination and social equality. Most of the mythologies surrounding American social mobility have been made obsolete by the heady ferment of the new global/information economy, but the university's stock in trade, a college diploma, has, if anything, appreciated in value as the future has become the quarry of literate "symbolic analysts" and administrators of what Mark Crispin Miller calls "the National Entertainment State."

With their prestige appreciating, universities have increasingly decided to make themselves over in the image of the corporation. As Bill Readings observed in his posthumously published study, *The University in Ruins*, the discourse of national culture that guided the founding of 19th-century universities has given way to a discourse of "excellence." Correspondingly, Readings argues, universities are no longer in the business of minting students into autonomous (though obedient) subjects of national cultures: instead, students are recast as consumers, and the administration of education becomes an exercise in Total Quality Management. Readings sees political opportunities for a meekly resurgent left in the university's corporatized "ruins," but a more forthright understanding would find that left politics in academia are, more or less by definition, ornamental. Since both culture and politics must rely on some rough consensus of shared purposes if they are not merely to shrink into ever-more irrelevant self-mythologization, the collapse of national culture as an animating ideal all but guarantees an exhaustion of meaningful intellectual resistance in American universities.

Consider the striking incoherence of the university in the labor problem that concerns it most directly: the sweated conditions of an enormous, and rapidly growing, cohort of entry-level university teachers. The university of excellence, after all, is a university of streamlined labor costs, and the customary attrition of professors through retirement or death is now being greeted in campuses

Grady Klein

across the land as an opportunity simply to abolish full professorships and transfer their teaching duties to graduate instructors and adjunct professors, who are often given per-semester stipends in the low four figures for work that is often more than full-time.

Such practices make a mockery of the trappings of institutional privilege in which university professors are accustomed to swathing themselves. And yet it is precisely those trappings — notably the institution of tenure, which (claims of sacrosanct academic freedom to the contrary notwithstanding) is the most politicized and solidarity-resistant accessory of university privilege — that continue to blind most university professors to the degraded working conditions visited on many of their putative peers.

The university of excellence has wasted little time sensing this weakness and moving into the vacuum. Today college executives are creating entire open-shop academic institutions: a new University of Arizona campus (called, in a winning tribute to the new global economy, Arizona International University) is proudly advertising its status as a "tenure-free" institution. Another Sunbelt concern, the University of Phoenix, is the nation's first for-profit institution of higher education. Specializing in the disbursement of professional credentials to already-working adults, the University of Phoenix — owned by a holding company called The Apollo Group and operating on 85 campuses in 11 states and Puerto Rico — now claims more than 32,000 students, making it the second-largest regionally accredited private university in the U.S., just behind NYU. In a truly excellent blurring of corporate and academic interests, AT&T has contracted the University of Phoenix to provide direct in-house instruction and training to employees. (Motorola is reportedly taking this process of identification one step further, by developing its own degree-granting postsecondary education program.) The University of Phoenix has also performed admirably as an investment. It began trading on Nasdaq in 1994, at a split-adjusted price of $2.06 a share; in March 1997 it traded at $27.25, a gain of 1,222 percent. Apollo Group CEO and University of Phoenix founder John G. Sperling, a former economics professor at San Jose State, is estimated to be worth some $300 million. Most traditional academics, of course, would dismiss such brave new institutional innovations as mere diploma mills, dealing in something distinctly other than "real" liberal arts pedagogy. But to do so is to gravely misread decades-long trends in higher education.

To grasp this point clearly, it's important to take stock of the internal economics of the university. As college education becomes one of the feverishly coveted accessories of the New Information Economy, colleges and universities, like most other social goods in America, are passing into a twilight of public access. A week after the Columbia teach-in, the New York Times reported that the College Board had found that for the fifth consecutive year overall college costs — tuition, expenses, and room and board — had increased by 5 percent, at twice the rate of inflation. The General Accounting Office reports that since 1980, tuition at public colleges has more than tripled, while household income increased by just 90 percent.

So as upper-income families blanch at the exorbitant costs of education at elite private colleges, they pack their scions off to the nation's more prestigious state schools: the University of Michigan, Berkeley, the University of Virginia. Russell Jacoby charts the steady "gentrification" of America's public universities in his study of the culture wars, Dogmatic Wisdom. At UCLA, more than 60 percent of incoming freshmen hailed from families with annual incomes of more than $60,000; 40 percent of these came from families with incomes greater than $100,000. Meanwhile students from lower middle-class families, who don't qualify for many forms of federal financial aid, decamp for community colleges — which now enroll more than half of the nation's incoming freshmen — or, astutely grasping the reading assignments they get from the bursar's office, throng to business programs and vocation-minded majors. In 1991, Jacoby reports, more than 250,000 of the more than 1 million bachelor's degress awarded in America went to business majors; foreign languages, by contrast, netted 12,000 majors, while philosophy and religion together totalled a mere 7,000. The American Academy of Liberal Arts Education reports an arresting sea change in the last generation of college students: Liberal-arts majors now comprise just 30 percent of all bachelor's degrees awarded nationwide, down from 70 percent in 1970.

At the bottom of the academic market, federal assistance, not surprisingly, is drying up. Pell Grants to disadvantaged students had been frozen for the better part of two decades before a recent Clinton initiative proposed modest increases in this year's budget. According to the College Board, Pell Grants have lost one-third of their value to inflation over the past 15 years. And as they have depreciated — and as fewer lower-income Americans attend college — they've fallen into increasing disuse: the grants showed a surplus of $506 million in fiscal 1996. Clinton plans to use this budget boon, with typical New Democrat élan, to underwrite his "targeted tax credits," which over-whelmingly favor the middle- and upper-middle-class families who are more likely to be able to afford college in the first place. As tuitions skyrocket, student loans are proliferating, plunging many unhirable humanities students into debt peonage. Students racked up $32.5 billion in debt in 1994, up 57 percent from 1992.

Against the backdrop of these trends, the tales of solidarity between academicians and the working class start to look more and more irrelevant — and, indeed, downright delusional. The American university is less than ever a refuge for the embattled aims of liberal education and social reform — and increasingly a clearinghouse of business hegemony, equal parts vocational shopping mall and corporate slush fund. The postures of radical intellectual vanguardism may be a beguiling intellectual hangover from the 1930s (or, worse yet, the 1960s), but they bear no resemblance to the experience of the vast majority of American students — and faculty — at the institutions left intellectuals serve. This doesn't mean, of course, that concerned left intellectuals should drop their loyalties and become obliging arbiters of excellence. It does mean that they should relinquish some long-cherished myths about the place of the university in American public life.

They could begin by shifting their gaze from the elite precincts of a place like Yale, which is not only a class anomaly in U.S. higher education, but a labor anomaly, in that it has two union locals on campus around which the graduate students' organizing efforts have hinged. Instead, consider a place like Long Island's Adelphi University — still a small and private liberal arts school, but one not nearly so cosseted from the logic of the market. Adelphi's story is an extreme case study, but it should serve as required reading for academics setting off for a career of freewheeling, Popular Front subversion.

THIS February, the New York State Board of Regents voted to dissolve the Board of Trustees at Adelphi University, only the fourth such action taken in the Regents' 212-year history. Like many private liberal arts schools, Adelphi had lately been experiencing declining enrollment and enacting a long series of tuition hikes. Neither prevented the 19-member Board of Trustees from approving a compensation package of more than $550,000 in salary, benefits, and deferred compensation to Adelphi President Peter Diamandopoulos last year, more than tripling his starting 1985 salary and making him the second highest-paid college president in the country. In addition the board graciously procured (and failed to report) a $1.15 million Manhattan condominium for Diamandopolous — which he had the option to purchase at a reduced rate of $900,000 — supplementing his university-supplied house, maintained at a cost of $100,000 a year in Garden City, Long Island.

Nor was Diamandopoulos' the only snout in the trough. One Adelphi trustee, insurance executive Ernesta Procope, raked in $1.2 million in commissions by arranging with Diamandopoulos to take on the school's liability insurance as she sat on the board; another, ad executive George Lois, took in $155,000 in commissions from the school's newspaper advertising campaign. (Other dismissed trustees included shipping magnate Peter Goulandris, one of the 10 wealthiest men in the world, Barnes & Noble CEO Leonard Riggio, splenetic right-wing Boston University President John Silber, who beat out Diamandopolous for the highest salary among American university presidents, and the neocon art critic Hilton Kramer.)

Adelphi had always been a capable dispenser of middle-class credentials, boasting solid programs in nursing and education. But Diamandopoulos saw the opportunity to line up serious money behind an inviting intellectual vanity project. The Olin Foundation, which fertilizes right-wing scholarly publications and faculty appointments across the nation to the tune of about $15 million a year, set aside $700,000 to fund an "Honors College" under Diamandopoulos' guidance at Adelphi that has sheltered neocon scholars such as *Partisan Review* editor Edith Kurzweil, revisionist Rosenberg historian Ronald Radosh, and Carnes Lord, a former national security adviser to Dan Quayle. (The Olin Foundation's president, former Nixon Treasury Secretary William E. Simon, was an honorary Adelphi trustee, but resigned last year, after the Foundation itself withdrew its Adelphi support in the wake of the Diamandopoulos controversy.)

To its credit, Adelphi's faculty union was instrumental in getting the state Board of Regents to dump the vultures on the Adelphi board. Yet the larger point remains: Professional academics — and entire departments and institutions, for that matter — are little more than interchangeable tokens in the transformation of American universities into virtual

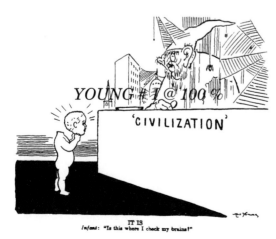

IT IS
Infant: "Is this where I check my brains!"

corporate theme parks.

The University of Rochester, the site of my own abortive graduate education and a way-station for Eastman-Kodak corporate largesse, boasts the lavish William E. Simon School of Business Administration (which infamously expelled an employee of Fuji, Kodak's leading global competitor, on the grounds that he might steal company secrets), a Bausch and Lomb science building, and all manner of Eastman institutional paraphernalia, from a music school to photography archives. The school also boasted a notable left-wing history department, but it would be fanciful to suppose that historians called any institutional shots.

Indeed, last year, Rochester's own downsize-and-damn-the-torpedoes administration — the college's president, Thomas Bradley, is a former bankruptcy lawyer — proposed eliminating the school's graduate history program altogether. Unprofitable graduate divisions such as anthropology and comparative literature had already fallen under the axe; graduate mathematics had already been eliminated — although after an unflattering *New York Times* story appeared about the decision, it was soon restored and "refocused" with 28 percent cuts in faculty. ("Refocusing" on a somewhat smaller scale was also the fate of Rochester's graduate programs in history, philosophy, mechanical engineering, and environmental sciences.) Meanwhile, the market-obsessed "empirical" social sciences could not have been more robust: Rochester continues to provide generous support to its high-profile "public choice" political science, behavioral psychology and neoclassical economics departments.

It is important to fix such cases clearly in mind when considering the rapprochement of labor and the academy, because today's left academics sometimes engage in a good deal of what earlier generations of more epistemologically confident leftists used to call "mystification" when they speak of the university and its aims. The essays collected in the Yale edition of *Social Text*, for example, all register varying degrees of astonishment at the thuggish labor practices of an institution supposedly steeped in traditions of critical inquiry, dissent and humanism. Understandably, most of the contributors want to prick the university's institutional conscience, and elicit anew the vision of campuses as hotbeds of dissent. As NYU historian Robin D. G. Kelley argues in his *Social Text* piece:

> After all, despite the resemblance, universities aren't exactly banks and investment firms. They have historically been places where alternatives to exploitation and oppression have been discussed and imagined in an institutional setting. They have been the sites of historic movements for social change precisely because the ostensible function of the university is to interrogate knowledge, society, history, and so on.

Such sentiments are, like the vision of a powerful strategic alliance between the AFL-CIO and America's university faculty, noble things to want to believe. They are, however, patently false. Small contingents of students — usually in shrinking humanities departments — will drink of these wellsprings of dissent; many more (in and out of the humanities) will see their colleges as porticoes to banks and investment firms. Most faculty are, if anything, more career-conscious than their students, and resigned to "interrogating" little beyond the odd controversial appointment or meaningless redoubt in the "culture wars." For that matter, on their side of the ledger, banks and investment firms tolerate many expressions of dissent and independent thought — as long as no one takes them seriously enough to consider acting on them. The situation in most American universities is precisely the same.

More revealing still are University of Illinois professor Michael Bérubé's reflections on the anti-GESO propaganda campaign conducted by Yale faculty and administration, in concert with the Modern Language Association. Bérubé, usually one of the most enthusiastic epigones of critspeak as revolutionary praxis, blasts the lies and doublespeak of antiunion faculty members, and subjects their pronouncements to close critical readings. He points out, as numerous other contributors do, the enormous profits and financial holdings of Yale, and scores the school's vicious, elitist and "Dickensian" campaign to wipe out HERE Locals 34 and 35.

But he can never bring himself to supply the simplest explanation for the intransigence of Yale's trustees and administration in the GESO campaign: No private school in America has recognized a graduate student union. Heretofore, all collective bargaining rights have been wrested from state universities; when graduate students are recognized as state employees, they can effectively go over the heads of administrations and win their bargaining rights from state legislatures and labor agencies. Yale is not standing firm purely out of its Dickensian greed — though that, of course, is an ancillary interest not to be discounted. It is acting out of institutional class interests that extend far beyond its leafy New Haven campus: If it were to cave in to GESO's demands, other organizing movements at other private universities would soon seize on the precedent and follow in its wake. Like any other business cartel, American private universities are standing pat to control their labor costs. Management's conduct in the Yale stalemate becomes especially intelligible as more than a curious "Dickensian" tic when viewed alongside a critical 1996 National Labor Relations Board ruling, which finally recognized graduate TAs as employees. That decision paves the way for collective bargaining rights if GESO can successfully get recognized by management as the bargaining agent for Yale's teaching assistants. Ergo, that recognition will be one of the very last things that Yale officialdom will extend, unless they are coerced by something a trifle more compelling than moral suasion and close readings of their many liberal-arts hypocrisies.

Rather than appealing to the elusive, and largely mythical, verities of liberal education — which Yale administrators believe in about as fervently as Coke executives think their product actually "adds life" — university faculties would be better occupied if they were forming alliances with unions and labor lawyers and "interrogating" ways they can organize across their individual campuses and challenge unpropitious conditions in private universities. They could look into the feasibility of lawsuits, assist in NLRB actions and investigate conflicts of interest among university board members. When finance scandals break out in one national political campaign, they are easily and correctly understood to grip all of our politics; yet when an Adelphi scandal or a Yale stalemate takes place, each is regarded as the byproduct of *sui generis* management styles.

Bérubé is aware of the gap between the successful organizing drives at public institutions and the bitterly stalemated one at Yale. But significantly, he chalks it up to Yale's generalized institutional culture of "elitism," instead of a brute conflict of interests. Faculty defenders of the administration's stand-pat labor policies, in Bérubé's account, regard schools with graduate-student unions as "plebeian, inferior"; they object to GESO's affiliation with Locals 34 and 35 because the latter are "smelly hotel and restaurant workers who don't know how a university works."

Elitism is no doubt real enough at Yale, but blaming the school's actions against GESO on the moral shortcomings of individual faculty is wildly misguided. The individual attitudes of antiunion university officials reflect, rather than inform, the labor agenda of Yale University. If administrators and faculty were to become suddenly nicer, or less elitist, the situation of graduate students and cafeteria and maintenance workers would change not at all.

Blindspots such as this tendency to personalize the Yale struggle are more than symptoms of that notorious academic misapprehension of "real world" relations of power. For some time, American politics generally, and academic left politics most particularly, has been trapped by a fatal reflex to recast questions of class as questions of culture. It is not too great an exaggeration to label this habit of mind a compulsion.

The Columbia teach-in provided a singularly instructive case study in the compulsion. Confronted over and over again with matters of inequality — declining living standards, the upward redistribution of wealth, the desperate need to revitalize the stagnant-to-declining state of organized labor, the workplace, and the welfare state, as well as the arid, depoliticized character of our intellectual life — speakers at the event made some sympathetic noises, but rushed with alacrity to the familiar, reassuring question of who in any given room benefits and suffers from which form of overarching cultural oppression. Hence the angry buzz when Harvard sociologist Orlando Patterson urged a rethinking of immigration policies. Hence the celebrated showdown between University of Virginia philosopher Richard Rorty and *Nation* columnist

Katha Pollitt over the New Left's role in abetting labor's decline, or the kindred, familiar face-off between Kelley and fellow NYU professor Todd Gitlin over identity politics.

Consider in this connection the curious notion of "classism." This locution (popularized in Herbert Gans' *The War Against the Poor*, but circulated widely among most *au courant* academicians) seeks to downgrade class antagonism — a conflict of material interests and the basis for a more just distribution of wealth — into a question of enlightened sensitivity. The main problem between classes, as it turns out, is snobbery and, as with the other "isms" of race and sex, the remedy for "classism" is presumably a program of re-education, of patiently tutoring plutocrats, like their fellow race and gender oppressors, to abandon their folkways of benighted ignorance. Wealth need not be redistributed, if only diversity workshops are broadened.

There's still another force behind the academy's painstaking class-to-culture alchemy, and that, of course, has to do with one of the most jealously guarded sources of prestige among contemporary intellectuals: their bottomlessly self-regarding sense of their own subversiveness. Culture, after all, is the natural habitat of most members of the left professoriate, and they naturally regard it as the pre-eminent domain of political confrontation. This sort of fanciful vanguardism is as old as intellectuals, but in the hands of *Social Text* coeditor Andrew Ross, it takes on rather comical proportions. In his Yale essay, Ross refers briefly to the downsizing of faculties and the erosion of tenure and full-time employment among academics. Then he takes a deep breath and delivers this analysis:

> Add this economic pressure to the acute political siege of sectors of the humanities and social sciences via

the Right's media-oriented campaign against the political correctness of tenured radicals: the result is an extensive backlash against the generational revolt of the 1960s, which declared that universities could no longer be seen as reliable sources of legitimation for the values and actions of the corporate-military state....[T]he abdication, in state capitals and in Congress, of the political will to fund education is hardly disconnected from the efforts to squeeze the academic Left.

It's difficult to know how to respond to such preening rhetoric, except to patiently note its irrelevance. Would that the academic left were one-twentieth, or one-one-hundredth, as influential as Ross imagines. State legislatures withhold funding from faculties in the humanities and social sciences for the same reason they are short-shrifted at "right-sizing" institutions like the University of Rochester: They preside over departments with declining enrollments, in a culture where their educational benefit is deemed marginal.

Prattling about the "extensive backlash" directed at the "generational revolt of the 1960s" feeds, rather than combats, such perceptions.

Of course, none of this means that left academics should abandon their efforts to mobilize support behind Sweeney's AFL-CIO or their commitment to the struggles of GESO and Locals 34 and 35. It does mean, however, that if the academy is serious about embracing the agenda of labor, it should do so on labor's terms, and not its own. It should strive to emulate not just the broad social justice aims of the labor movement, but the very particular ways in which labor has propagated a more democratic culture — the documentary film and scholarship efforts of 1199, a union of hospital and healthcare workers, or the successful *Detroit Sunday Journal* published by the striking employees of Detroit's two dailies. Such breakthroughs in union culture, fragile though they may be, are infinitely more valuable instances of political education than the interminable diversions of the culture wars.

Just wrapping its institutional brain

around this fundamental point should keep the American professoriate occupied for some time. One indication of just how far professional academics will have to go is again supplied by Ross, who felt compelled to remind readers of his *Social Text* piece that, no, unions are not "exclusively preoccupied with bread-and-butter issues" and, more condescendingly, that "it is wrong to think of unions as antithetical to the spirit of education." (Just imagine the tumult that would have occurred at the Columbia teach-in if John Sweeney were to have calmly mused in an aside, "Well, maybe not all college faculty are middle-management toadies, after all.")

Moreover, despite such caveats, Ross can't restrain himself from addressing his fellow left intellectuals in the very next paragraph as deferential, impressionable students. And the advice he offers them is singularly bad. "If there is going to be a graduate union at universities like Yale, why not aim for an expansive, utopian union with a broad intellectual role to play on and off campus?" Stumbling into the very "bread-and-butter" stereotype he had tried meekly to fend off a few sentences back, he continues:

> Don't settle for a technocratic bargaining unit, whose only mandate is the protection of its students' material concerns. Make sure that it also has some voice in curricular reform and in faculty recruitment, and that it is set up to sponsor and broker debates about academic matters. These must include issues related to the vocational structure of graduate education. Make sure, in other words, that your union has something to say, because a union with nothing to say in the long run may be a union not worth having.

Consider how ruinous this sort of strategy would be. For the moment, of course, students juggling enormous teaching loads on sub-living wages would be achieving a tremendous breakthrough to win mere "protection" of their "material concerns." Moreover, it is entirely appropriate for Yale grad students — and Americans in general — to reverse the polarity of Ross's sage advice and ask simply, "What have the culture wars done for me lately?" Why on earth should anyone be exercised over "curricular reform" when the vast majority of American universities don't have curricular requirements in the first place? Why should fledgling unions steer into the quagmires of "faculty recruitment" or the sort of identity-obsessed "academic matters" Ross champions when such melees will only, at best, distract and divide their memberships?

More important, if intellectuals intend to make class politics more than just another specialty on their CVs, they sorely need to re-examine the academy's entire system of governance, and the accelerating inequalities in the distribution of higher education. Writing almost 80 years ago, Thorstein Veblen argued for the abolition of university boards of trustees and college presidents — or, as he called them, "captains of erudition." No other Western country had bothered to establish college presidencies, he noted; and academic boards and executives alike are "quite useless to the university" even "for any businesslike purpose." Modeled on earlier, ecclesiastical systems of university governance, boards functioned, in Veblen's view, chiefly to shore up members' prestige by granting them the powers to enforce intellectual conformity and generate publicity for themselves via "a bootless meddling in academic affairs they do not understand."

Veblen's critique has grown more urgent with time, as a case like Adelphi's amply demonstrates. Yet the academic left, despite its loving characterization of itself as an embattled, victimized minority of opinion, won't advance anything resembling such an analysis. Few left academics would even entertain the notion of taking a critical look at sacrosanct institutions like tenure in light of what unions may have to teach them. And the reform that would most obviously bring higher education in line with the principles of social democracy — the nationalization of American universities into a publicly administered system, as is the common Western European model — is not even up for discussion.

Nor is it hard to understand why: Too much is at stake for the professoriate in the preservation of the current regime of university management. The institutional prestige they derive from present arrangements — as well as the distant allure of superstar six-figure incomes at name institutions — is infinitely more powerful than the drudge work of piecing together class solidarity, which is the political equivalent of grading your own blue books. And meanwhile, left academics are institutionally rewarded for practicing a nonthreatening, diversionary cultural politics that produces nothing but meandering, tail-chasing arguments and publishing opportunities. The rewards for such activities are no longer confined, by the way, to the towers of Ivory: Andrew Ross recently roped in a six-figure advance from Ballantine — one of the many jewels in the crown of right-wing publishing mogul S. I. Newhouse — for a book to be based on his forthcoming move to Disney's planned community of Celebration, Florida. (The opus will presumably be something other than a diary of Ross's efforts to organize the unorganized imagineers who make the Magic Kingdom hum.)

For all the beguiling talk of a Popular Front redux, immersing professors, teaching assistants, and unions into an undifferentiated tide of New Deal social democracy, some preliminary spadework needs to be attended to. Until academics start to reckon with the social forces that have made American colleges into bastions of privilege and business culture, they will have done little to advance the cause of working Americans. Teach-ins and high-profile publications may get all sorts of press attention, but the real rebirth of labor politics in the academy should start with four simple words: Solidarity begins at home.

The Skin Sellers

Stepan Chapman

DERMALI was once a tiny nation in the Balkans. It no longer exists. But its culture lives on among the Dermalian-Americans.

In the Twenties, after the Dermalian economy had been smashed by The Great War, six of my eight great-grandparents emigrated to the United States and settled in three of the larger American cities, where bilingual enclaves of our people were forming.

That makes me a fourth-generation D.-A. by blood. But I've assimilated pretty thoroughly. I know exactly five words of Dermish, and I dance no Dermalian folk dances. My father is another story.

When an ethnic group jumps into the Melting Pot, the breadwinners sometimes gravitate to a particular profession. Irishmen often joined police departments; many Jews opened up tailor shops; and lots of Chinese found work at laundries. Similarly, a large contingent of immigrant Dermalians snagged jobs as hospital orderlies.

There are various theories to explain this demographic quirk. One theory holds that Dermalian men tend to be quiet, serious, and clean — traits that are valued in hospital orderlies. An orderly is essentially a janitor, but he's a glorified janitor, a janitor in a sterile, white uniform and rubber-soled shoes.

The men of my grandfather's generation were intensely proud of their work. They hoped that someday their grandsons might go to training colleges and become registered nurses.

Their faction got control of a national labor union, and nepotism did the rest. Fathers wangled orderly jobs for more and more sons, until young D.-A.s were mopping the floors of all the major hospitals.

At the onset of World War II, every American urban center included a clean, quiet neighborhood full of clean, quiet Dermalian families, all raising their children to speak English. The working men rode buses to their hospitals at all hours, and dreamed of acquiring used cars.

During the postwar period, blood transfusions became commonplace, and many new blood banks were established. Dermalian-American orderlies saw that nurses were drawing blood from various lowlifes and paying out good money for the privilege. Reasoning that their blood was as red as any other American's, many orderlies began to sell their blood on weekends, to supplement their incomes and to make life easier for their wives.

More recently, in the era of kidney transplants and artificial knees, the D.-A. community embarked upon a whole new profession, moving from blood donorship to the next logical level. They started selling their skins. Not all at once, of course, but in strips.

The strips are usually removed at burn wards, for grafting purposes. The skin is rendered universally graftable by means of patented pharmaceutical viruses, which eat the chromosomes right out of the ectodermal nucleoplasms.

Blood is worth peanuts, compared to skin. If a man is a fast healer, he can make a bundle selling his skin. Enterprising D.-A.s left their hospitals and started working out of their apartments as private contractors. They would visit burn wards or cosmetic surgery clinics for removals and then recuperate at home.

My father's generation saw the skin profession as a brave new world of economic opportunity. The demand for skin had created a seller's market.

But they had to put up with a few unsightly side effects. The skin grows back, but the new skin never perfectly matches the skin around it. First a strip grows back coarse and hairy. Chimp skin, they call it. Then it begins to grow back pale and smooth and waxen — corpse skin. A skin seller comes to resemble a patchwork quilt. It takes some getting used to.

Dermalian-Americans became a highly visible minority. Women of other ethnicities shunned the skin sellers. Intermarriage with other groups, formerly on the rise, took a downswing. But Dermalian women have grown accustomed to piebald complexions. When a Dermalian woman spots a guy in a tank top, his arms all pink and red and white, she doesn't think, *How gross!* She thinks, *Ah! A good provider.*

Nonetheless, the men of my generation have turned against the practice. We've seen the long-term health problems involved. The skin keeps growing back, yes, but thinner and thinner, more and more varicose and translucent. And numbness sets in.

A skin seller who gets greedy and overworks himself can wind up as a very young corpse and a very unsightly one, usually in a closed casket.

Consider the case of my father. He's sold skin all his life. I went into tax accounting,

and he's never forgiven me. He wanted me to follow in his footsteps.

The two of us have been getting into fights over this ever since I was in high school. It started when I refused to sell leg strips for a summer job. We said some ugly things that day.

"It's just a few hunks off your butt and thighs!" he protested. "It's nothing! Who's going to notice? You just wear long pants."

"Dad, when was the last time you went to a *beach?*"

He snorted. "Dermalians don't go to those places."

"All my friends do."

"What a sissy you are. What vanity! Don't be so concerned with surfaces."

"Dad, it isn't *healthy. Look* at yourself for Christ's sake!"

"Watch your mouth," he told me. "Your mother is in the kitchen."

These arguments have continued. I scold my father for making unnecessary sacrifices, and he reminds me that his hide put me through college.

Whenever I visit him, he's lying in bed,

regrowing. In pajamas, he looks like a damned *science project*. Mom wishes that I'd just stay away. But I have to get through to him. He won't be around much longer.

For the last month, Dad's been in a hospital. Some kind of fungus has got under his skin, what's left of it. They've got him in a ward that smells of saline baths and pusy gauze. He shares a row of beds with a bunch of poor bastards who have skin cancer or UV burns. The same people who've been buying Dad's skin all these years — them or their insurance companies.

He lies on bleached bedsheets, all moist and raw, like skinned meat waiting for the butcher. There ought to be a buzzard perched on his headboard.

I went there today and pleaded with him one last time.

"Look, Dad, I *know* that you did this for your wife and your kids. But it's *ruined* you. And you didn't have to do it! You sold yourself for money!"

"So what?" he said. "That's how America works, chum. That's what made America strong. We'll do *anything* for a price. You wouldn't know about that, Mr. Fancy-Pants College Boy."

"Dad, you threw away your future."

"What horse shit! You're just ashamed of me. You're like those bleeding-heart liberals who want to outlaw the automobile just because of some holes in the ozone layer. You call that *progress?!*"

"Dad, that's not a fair comparison. We're talking about a part of your *body*."

"Get out of here," he told me. "You don't belong here. I can't stand the sight of you."

There was no more to say. I rode an elevator to the lobby.

I put on my pith helmet and my plastic UV shroud. I pushed through the hospital's revolving door. I walked to my car in the deathly white sunlight.

It was over 120 Fahrenheit in Albuquerque. The ultraviolet index was far into the Red Zone. It had stayed in the Red for two weeks. It showed no signs of falling.

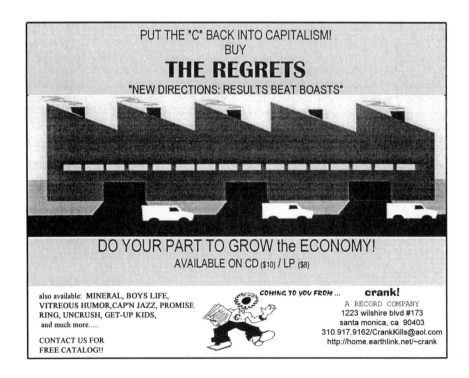

What the Frick

Dan Bischoff

Y ou couldn't help noticing the three prep school kids lounging outside the entrance to the Frick Museum at Fifth Avenue and 71st Street. It was a white-knuckle cold day, not yet spring, and they were wearing nothing but tweed jackets, khakis, and long mufflers. I was on my way for a behind-the-scenes tour of the upstairs rooms of the Frick, including the private family quarters — *terra incognita* to museum-goers, since the second floor is always roped off for staff only — so I slowed down when I heard them talking about the people who once had lived inside.

"You know, this guy Henry Clay Frick was a real bastard," one said, taking a drag on a cigarette. "He had all this money, but he got it off the backs of his workers. He was really mean to labor. So this was all built with tainted money."

At first, nobody replied to that, but as I passed them to walk up the little granite stairs and they stood to follow me in, I heard another kid say, "Well, if it's great art, what the frick?"

Henry Clay Frick would have been pleased by that remark. Labor erects few monuments in America, but capitalists sow them like teeth wherever they live; and few of capital's monuments are more eloquent or more imposing than the sprawling granite mansion built here in 1913, for 4 million pre-inflation dollars, by the victor in the famous Homestead steel lockout.

Today it houses the Frick Collection and library, but it was built as a home. And like most of the palaces of America's plutocracy, its architecture is stamped with the class assumptions of its occupants — down to details like the polished mahogany veneer on doors facing the Frick family quarters, and the

knotty pine on the side facing the servants'.

Well, the etiquette of live-in service is lost on most of us now, but clearly there are still powerful ghosts to be exorcised around the Frick name. To take the full measure of the Fifth Avenue palace, you need to know something about Frick's Pittsburgh mansion, Clayton, a massive turreted affair on the corner of Penn and Homewood Avenues along what used to be called Millionaires' Row. The two Frick houses tell a story not only of the evolution of one man's taste but of capital itself, from purely local influence to global barony — an evolution that was accelerated by the crushing defeat Frick imposed on the nascent union movement at Homestead in the summer of 1892.

The Homestead battle is famous not just because it was such a devastating defeat — ending as it did all hope for unionization of the steel industry for more than 40 years — but because it marked a turning point in the relationship between labor and capital, just like Ronald Reagan's dismissal of PATCO, the air traffic controllers' union, in 1981. Homestead forever associated Frick's name with both the use of immigrant laborers as scabs and mortal violence.

Homestead was a model mill in the vast metalworking complex surrounding Pittsburgh, most of which was owned 100 years ago by Carnegie Steel. Frick, the dour scion of a landowning family of Pennsylvania Mennonites, held a monopoly on the supply of coke, a byproduct of partially burned coal that was essential in the making of steel. Through his control of the coke fields along the Youghigheny River he had risen to be leading partner and executive director of Carnegie Steel, thereby taking charge of Homestead.

Sooty enough to turn the ground around them ash black for miles (somebody had written in the margin of my library copy of Samuel Schreiner's biography of Frick, "There's a reason they call it Pittsburgh"), the mills were dangerous caldrons of white-hot metal and sulphurous fumes. Even the social Darwinist Herbert Spencer said that a week in the Pittsburgh mills would be enough to make "a sane man commit suicide."

The industrialists of the 1870s and Eighties had achieved a kind of labor peace in this hell by buying off the skilled trade unions, and at the Homestead plant in particular, the Amalgamated Association of Iron and Steel Workers had won not only some control of working conditions in the plant but a hand in promotion decisions. What's more, the Amalgamated all but controlled the politics of the town of Homestead, electing a mayor who spoke with pride of labor's role in creating the most efficient steel mill in the world. So persuasive was the American myth of hard work's ultimate value that the union truly believed that it, too, had some claim of ownership in the mill.

Henry Clay Frick didn't see it that way. A proponent of the theory that modern industrial combines must expand their control in all areas of their activities through the latest in scientific advances, Frick championed new processes that would reduce costs by eliminating skilled labor. The cheapest way to go about the change, he figured, would be to provoke a strike, shut down the mill for a few months, and then bring in Hungarian and Polish immigrants to replace the union. In 1892, he built a palisade topped with barbed wire all around the mill, and prepared to do just that.

After a bizarre battle involving boatloads of Pinkerton hired-guns had left 10 dead and 60 wounded—and after the state militia had intervened to save Frick's ass—the union was smashed, and the families that had thrown in their lot with it lost not just their jobs but their homes.

Frick was a punctilious man with a trim, spade-like beard, always impeccably dressed. Throughout the violence, he continued to commute from Clayton to his second-floor office downtown, keeping to his routine like clockwork. Today, Clayton has been restored as a museum dedicated to a wealthy family's private way of life in the high Nineties, complete with children's games laid out on tables and a landscape by a local Pennsylvania artist, George Hetzel, which was the first acquisition

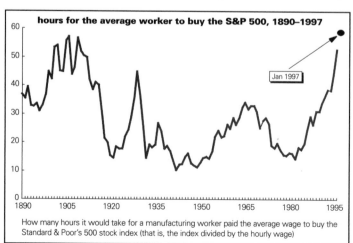

hours for the average worker to buy the S&P 500, 1890–1997

Jan 1997

How many hours it would take for a manufacturing worker paid the average wage to buy the Standard & Poor's 500 stock index (that is, the index divided by the hourly wage)

in the Frick Collection. The building is a hodgepodge of ambitious styles, each element grasping for grandeur in some unconnected way. The facade is a poor copy of a French chateau; here rises a round turret; there a square one. The interior is similarly incoherent, a Peter Pan riot of Tiffany glass, dark woodwork, hideaway staircases, patterned parquet, and small, dark rooms rambling here and there.

O NE Saturday afternoon in July, after the Pennsylvania militia had restored order in the mills, Frick had come in from Clayton to his office when a Russian anarchist named Alexander Berkman burst in and shot him twice in the neck. In the ensuing struggle, Berkman stabbed Frick in the back and both legs before he was subdued.

Several doctors appeared and Frick, bleeding profusely and without benefit of anesthetic, allowed himself to be probed, even helping to guide the doctors' instruments to the lodged bullets with his own hands. He dictated cables while they fussed with the bandages, and stayed at work until seven in the evening, completing an important loan instrument, before heading back to Clayton.

He became a hero to the upper classes forever after that, and you would have thought the general American public might have at least given him credit for grit. But another brutal incident prevented that favorite American delusion from getting off the ground. On hearing the news that Frick had been shot, one of the soldiers guarding the mill at Homestead shouted "Hurrah for the man who shot him!", whereupon an officer had the offending private hung from a tent pole by his thumbs until his heartbeat grew so faint a surgeon ordered him taken down. The soldier never apologized, so he was given a dishonorable discharge, his head was half-shaved, and he was kicked out of camp in rags.

The soldier's treatment was such an obvious and immediate symbol of the new relationship between the classes in the United States that the popular press never really got around to giving Frick any laurels for his courage — if that's what refusing to leave your job with two bullets in your neck really is. For the next 20 years, Carnegie Steel reaped enormous profits from its ever-expanding, union-free mills, and the value of Frick's holdings skyrocketed. Slowly he switched from the mundane and local business of coke and steel to the ethereal, pure capitalism of banking and speculation, just like his protegé and fellow Pennsylvanian, Andrew Mellon. After a few years as a financier, he felt he should leave Pittsburgh for the city of financiers.

In an era when a million dollars was worth a million dollars, Frick controlled hundreds of millions. The $4 million cost of the mansion he built on Fifth Avenue in New York is easily worth twice the $40 million-plus Bill Gates is shelling out for his convention center of a house on Lake Washington in Seattle. Frick imported teams of Italian workmen to cut the stone, carve the moldings, and lay the hardwood floors. The public rooms in the Frick are hung with silks and lined with paintings, among them Rembrandts, Holbeins, Bellinis, Van Dykes, Vermeers — all housed on a scale reminiscent of the Tuscan villas and palaces Frick and Mellon toured in the summers. The architect who designed the National Gallery of Art in Washington, D.C., also did occasional additions to the Frick home.

You can still detect signs of family use downstairs, notably in the little mother-of-pearl buttons along the wainscoting labelled "kitchen" or "maid" or "butler." There is a unique self-playing organ in one wall, and press accounts of the period liked to picture Frick sitting alone under a Renaissance baldachin in one of his enormous galleries, listening to the automatic organ play.

Maybe it happened that way, but the

private rooms suggest it did not. There was magnificence here, too — a cedar-lined closet that is big enough to be a bedroom, and a Titanic-era pool table, elaborately carved, standing next to a private, teak-lined bowling alley with leather pads for backstops (unfortunately, this was a game Frick could not play without servants to set the pins and roll back the balls). Walls are covered with heavy damask, and mantels are hung with fruit and birds cut in dense relief from oak. The windows are too small and deep-cut to be really bright. The ceilings are no more than eleven feet high (you feel like ducking after the airiness downstairs) and no room would seem out of scale for a decent middle-class home today. The family furniture that remains is dark and sturdy-looking but not jaw-dropping. There are no columns or rooftop gardens, just solid, rectangular, Protestant rooms that look out onto Central Park.

The servants' quarters, though, are like dorm rooms in a community college, and some, downstairs by the kitchen, have walls lined with white tile — an antiseptic innovation of which Frick was quite proud, but which no doubt made the chauffeurs and cooks feel like they were sleeping in a bedpan.

Compared to his manse in Pittsburgh, though, the Frick house in New York is a revelation, a tableau of the newly global power of American capital in the years before World War I. Here the European references were executed by actual Europeans, imported from Italy, Britain, and France for the task. The older building's haphazard feel and provincial pretensions give way to coherence and genuine sophistication; its almost desperate social aspirations to a confident invocation of Europe, where the classes knew their places and stayed put. This building is about power, global, rational, and remorseless. It also feels a little like a mausoleum. But the only thing that's buried here is Frick's reputation, which all the oil paints of Europe can't seem to beautify.

X Minus X

Even when your friend, the radio, is still; even when her
    dream, the magazine, is finished; even when his life, the
    ticker, is silent; even when their destiny, the boulevard,
    is bare;
And after that paradise, the dance-hall, is closed; after that
    theater, the clinic, is dark,

Still there will be your desire, and hers, and his hopes and
    theirs
Your laughter, their laughter,
Your curse and his curse, her reward and their reward, their
    dismay and his dismay and her dismay and yours—

Even when your enemy, the collector, is dead; even when
    your counsellor, the salesman, is sleeping; even when
    your sweetheart, the movie queen, has spoken; even
    when your friend, the magnate, is gone.

— Kenneth Fearing
(Originally published as "Rialto Equation" in *Dynamo: A
Journal of Revolutionary Poetry*, January 1934)

Bread and Roses and Now, Circuses, Too!

Frances Reed

THE Lawrence textile strike of 1912 — a defining moment in the history of the anarcho-syndicalist Industrial Workers of the World — is now commemorated by the Massachusetts State Parks. The victory of the Lawrence workers is now brought to us "courtesy of the Yankee Technology Corporation." Full security luxury condos loom high above the well-endowed heritage museum of this "City of Workers." But even against this backdrop of corporate paternalism, the "Bread and Roses" strike continues to resonate. Standing amid the empty paraphernalia of contemporary business civilization, it helps to remember that in 1912, the fat mill owners, however absurd they may appear now, must have seemed as omnipotent as information capitalism does today.

The workers' rebellion is still the most important event in Lawrence history, and the town's heritage museum tells the story with impressive candor. Inside you can trace the path of multiple immigrant groups to Lawrence or watch a video of the famous strike. An enormous painting of thousands of striking workers surrounded by militia men hangs in the foyer. The windows of the museum look out onto the still-intimidating mills, brick leviathans towering above the icy Merrimack River. Even today, the biting winter air evokes the desperation the workers must have felt on that frigid January day in 1912 when they marched out of the Lawrence Wood Mill, entreating others to follow. They endured freezing temperatures, prejudice, and violence, all to win a wage increase of 2¢ an hour — an amount that now seems more symbolic than monetary.

Lawrence was then and remains today a city of immigrants. One of the first "planned communities," this capitalist utopia was erected by wealthy Boston investors in 1845 complete with housing, schools, churches, and a large common. It was designed to make the wealthy investors wealthier while also affording them a sense of paternalistic satisfaction. Over the next 50 years immigrants from as many as 40 different ethnic groups came to Lawrence looking for a better life. What they found instead were long hours, low wages, disease, and death. Nevertheless, a steady stream continued to pour into this factory town, lured by propaganda cartoons distributed throughout Europe of workers leaving the mills with baskets full of money. As the population increased, living conditions became even more squalid, overcrowded and unhygienic. The infant mortality rate among Lawrence workers was 172 per 1,000. When a typhoid epidemic spread by polluted river water ravaged the city's poor in the 1890s, the mill owners installed a purifying system and passed the expense on to the workers.

During these crucial years wages were so low that no family could exist on just one. Women and children, though paid only $6 a week to a man's $8.76, were forced into the mills and actually became the majority of the Lawrence workforce. On the backs of these men, women and children William Wood's American Woolen Co. and others of its ilk built a textile empire, and by 1910 Lawrence was the nation's leader in the production of woolens. Claiming to "Weave the World's Worsted with the Waters of the Merrimack," the mill owners prospered.

Then in January 1912, Massachusetts passed a reform measure that limited the hours women and children could work to 54 hours a week. In response, the mill owners slashed these "unskilled" workers' already minimal weekly wages. When the workers learned of the pay cut, a spontaneous wave of anger rippled through the mills. A group of Polish women walked out immediately. The next morning, an irate group of Italians ran through the mills, destroying machinery, throwing ice and rocks at the windows, and shouting for others to join them on strike. By evening 10,000 had walked out, and by week's end 15,000 more joined them. I.W.W. strike leader Joseph Ettor and syndicalist poet Arturo Giovannitti rushed into town to support the strike, and a frightened Mayor Scanlon called out 250 local militia. The fight for bread and roses had begun.

Most of the mill workers were not unionized when they walked off their jobs. Their different cultures, religions and languages often got in the way of building solidarity. The mill's craft unionists, made up of skilled workers from the more acculturated, or "Americanized," immigrant groups, actually opposed the strike. But by excluding the "unskilled foreigners" from their ranks, craft unions like the United Textile Workers had left the majority of the Lawrence workforce with no organized defense when wages were cut.

The I.W.W., of course, had no such qualms, organizing anyone who worked, including women, minorities, and immigrants. Though the local branch had only about 300 members at the time (only one woman among them), after the January walkout the membership grew to upwards of 16,000. I.W.W. bigshots Elizabeth Gurley Flynn and Big Bill Haywood came to Lawrence to fire the cause with incendiary speeches. The workers demanded a wage increase, overtime pay, workplace reforms, and no discrimination against strikers. They organized, set up soup kitchens, staged rallies, and marched through the streets singing the *Internationale* and shouting "give us bread, and roses too." This now-famous slogan meant "we fight not only for subsistence, but for dignity and beauty as well." As the famous I.W.W. song goes: "Hearts starve as well as bodies; give us bread, but give us roses!"

The police, the mill owners, and the Massachusetts militia responded with violence. They turned hoses of icy water on marchers, planted dynamite to frame the strike leaders, and clubbed and beat women and children. Harvard students were given course credit for serving in the militia. Before long Lawrence become a scene of astonishing official violence and bizarre outrages of justice. On January 29, only two weeks into the battle, a local policeman shot and killed a young woman striker during a scuffle between marchers and militia. A few days later, I.W.W. strike leaders Ettor and Giovannitti were framed and arrested as co-conspirators in her murder. But the Lawrence strikers did not succumb; instead they decided to dramatize the violence by sending their children out of town for the duration. The plans for a "children's exodus" infuriated the mill owners, and the city fathers decreed that no child could leave Lawrence without written parental consent. Later, they forbade any children to leave, no matter what. Despite this order, on February 24, 200 children showed up with their parents at the town train station to meet their escorts out of the city. They were met instead by the clubs and fists of the local police.

Jailing Wobbly agitators was one thing; cops beating children was quite another. Support for the workers began to pour in from all corners. President Taft ordered the Bureau of Labor to investigate conditions at Lawrence. Two weeks later, on March 12, the American Woolen Co. agreed to meet the workers' demands across the board.

Under today's January sky Bostoners in bright jogging suits drive up to Lawrence to shop in the factory outlet stores housed in the old mills. They buy Polarfleece from Malden Mills, women's separates, and Silver Sweet Candies. A run-down building on Mill St. still bears the name "AMERICAN WOOLEN CO." emblazoned across its stone pediment. Out from the broken upper windows you can hear a local punk band rehearsing in what was once, perhaps, the office of William Wood. Immigrants still move here looking for a better life, but now they come from Latin American and Southeast Asia. You can eat at Cafe Azteca across from the Campagnone Common, the grassy park where the strike leaders held their rallies and gave their rousing speeches. For the last 12 years Lawrence has celebrated the Bread and Roses strike every Labor Day with a city-wide festival. 15,000 residents join together to eat, dance, socialize, remember, and re-enact the textile worker's victory. One can only imagine what goes through their heads as they mimic the militancy of the 1912 battle, as they march in the warmth of a late-century May Day shouting: "Give us bread, but give us roses too!"

Distinguo

Freedom, yes, but a Freedom combed and curled,
A safe, tame Freedom, eating from the hand,
A Freedom which will lie down at command,
Not this wild wench whose scarlet flag unfurled
Threatens our cozy, comfortable world
With voice like thunder echoing through the land,
Who tramps the highway with her ragged band
Of va-nu-pieds from the depths upwhirled.
God save us from her—We've no use for kings,
Crowns are obnoxious, scepters are taboo,
But lawyers, plutocrats, are sacred things.
Touch not the Black Coat, lest you should undo
The very woof of life and fling destroyed,
Our spinning earth to chaos and the void.

— Lizinka Campbell Turner
(Originally published in *The Liberator*, May 1918)

Strike City, Miss.

Hunter Kennedy

IT'S not that far from Midnight, Mississippi or Panther Burn. All it's got is a street sign that says Strike City Road. You would miss it if you weren't headed to a wedding deep in the Delta and knew to turn off Highway 82 on a road flanked by bonfires. You wouldn't even give that sign a second thought if your guide, a local cotton planter, hadn't pointed it out to you. This is what he has told you. Some folks came down from Chicago or New York to organize the black farm workers. The organizers visited different farms to see the conditions of the workers, and they convinced the men on Mr. A. L. Andrews' place that they had a bad deal and should strike. This was the Sixties, at a time when a black man made $8 a day chopping cotton. So they struck. It was the height of the summer, and when the men walked out, they thought they had Andrews in a bind. Problem was, they lived in Andrews' houses. Andrews kicked them off the property and hired the white men he needed the next day. The organizers sent $10,000 to build housing for the strikers, and Strike City was born.

I decide to see Strike City for myself.

Tucked off of the road, Strike City takes half a minute to drive through. Two dogs fight at the entrance. A whitewashed meeting house sits at the center of the horseshoe, its windows painted white. A cinderblock two-story building, half of which is painted and lived in, the other half blackened by flames, faces the meeting house. A church waits at the end of the loop. Re-bar cages guard the brand-new air conditioning units behind the chapel, which is sparsely decorated in blue tinsel. There would be no midnight theft of such a hard-won luxury. Other objects decorating the grounds of Strike City are not so jealously guarded. Discarded playground equipment lies heaped in the horseshoe, overrun by dry weeds. Junked cars rust without a whimper, barricading the only pair of houses. A dented trailer stands nakedly between Strike City and the fallow fields. Driving this loop, you wonder where these people are now. Not a face comes to the window, and the questions dangle, unanswered. Strike City may not appear on any maps, but you know Mr. A. L. Andrews never forgot about this place.

Cram Your Spam

Peter Rachleff

FOR more than three years in the mid-1980s, grassroots union activists and their supporters waged a remarkable campaign against the George A. Hormel Company of Austin, Minnesota. The high point of the struggle was a 10-month strike by Local P-9 of the United Food and Commercial Workers (UFCW). The strike lasted from August 1985 to June 1986, and ended when the UFCW international leadership placed P-9 in trusteeship and signed a contract capitulating to most of the company's terms, including the permanent replacement of strikers. Well before the beginning of the strike, local activists had energized union members and their families, reached out for support from other trade unionists, and launched a corporate campaign against Hormel and its financial backers. For more than a year after the strike, these activists continued to promote a boycott of Hormel products and to encourage other meatpacking workers to stand up to their international union.

This struggle became a central symbol of rank-and-file workers' resistance to management demands for concessions in the 1980s and appeared, at its height, to be on the verge of galvanizing a renewal of the American labor movement. In the end, the combined powers of the international union bureaucracy (with the support of the AFL-CIO hierarchy), the state and its National Guard, the Hormel Company and its backers, and the media, were able to crush the local.

From the start, the Hormel struggle was as much a cultural conflict as a political one. P-9 had to fight to have its point of view represented at all, much less to get a fair hearing. During the strike, Austin's school board forbade teachers to discuss the conflict in their classrooms. Once the strike was over, opponents wasted little time seeking to eradicate any traces of it from the media and popular memory. Local radio, television, and newspapers eagerly announced the end of the strike in the summer of 1986 and hurriedly dropped a blackout curtain on all continuing efforts by strikers and their supporters. After taking control of the Austin union hall in the summer of 1986, the UFCW's trustees sandblasted a 16-by-80-foot mural that had been painted by more than 100 rank-and-filers. This stunning representation of the strike's place in labor history was wiped off the face of the hall's exterior brick wall.

The easiest way to obliterate popular memory of the strike, of course, was simply to get rid of the workers. Once they signed the contract, workers found out that the company wasn't planning on calling back any of the 1,000 remaining P-9 strikers and that only 300 of them would be placed on a recall list at all. Moreover, a clause in the contract allowed the company to discharge from this recall list any worker who actively advocated a boycott of Hormel products. Other workers were told to take retirement if eligible, or to take out "withdrawal" cards from the union. Many of the most committed rank-and-filers and strike activists were forced to leave town in a search for employment.

Given the power of these forces, it is amazing that any memory of the struggle was kept alive at all. But it was.

P-9 activists who left Austin took their experiences, memories, and commitments with them. Some headed to the Twin Cities or other nearby communities, while others moved farther away. Several of them soon emerged as union activists in their new workplaces. They and others found new niches for activism in the labor movement.

In the Twin Cities, P-9 supporters shifted gears into a wider effort to bring education, labor history, and militant strategies into the labor movement. Some launched the St. Paul Labor Speakers Club, which has sponsored a public educational forum once a month for the past 10 years, building a mailing list of 1,600 local union activists and supporters. In the early 1990s, Twin Cities activists organized the Meeting the Challenge Committee, which has sponsored five annual educational conferences and organized a variety of social events. They also engaged in solidarity work, organizing picket-line support for local strikes and fundraising for the locked-out Staley workers in Decatur, Illinois.

In Austin, retirees, former P-9ers and their families also kept their story alive. In July 1987, when the Hormel Company and the Austin city government turned the 4th of July into "Spam Days," these activists responded with a counter-celebration of "Cram-Your-Spam Days." They marked their lawns with crosses bearing the names of replaced strikers, and they maintained a visible (and noisy) presence at the local festivities. They

have continued to meet weekly as the United Support Group.

Their most public expression came in August 1995, when P-9 veterans organized a series of events to mark the tenth anniversary of the beginning of the strike. They held a parade and a rally that brought exiled activists back to town, together with former supporters and other people who had more recently learned about the struggle. The Hormel Company was so concerned about the anniversary celebration that it scheduled work on both Saturday and Sunday for the first time in more than a year. Some workers skipped work nonetheless.

In December 1992, a group of former strikers who had finally been called back to work regained control of the local union from the scabs who had held office since the end of the strike. While they remain caught between the company and the international union, they have have rebuilt the local and undone some of the damage done during the trusteeship.

Like many other notable struggles in American labor history, the Hormel strike may have been defeated. But the strikers never became defeatist, never assumed the role of victims. They continue to hold their heads high and contribute to the vital project of the rebuilding of the labor movement. And their story has been kept alive.

Asbestos

Knowing (as John did) nothing of the way
men act when men are roused from lethargy,
and having nothing (as John had) to say
to those he saw were starving just as he

starved, John was like a workhorse. Day by day
he saw his sweat cement the granite tower
(the edifice his bone had built), to stay
listless as ever, older every hour.

John's deathbed is a curious affair:
the posts are made of bone, the spring of nerves,
the mattress bleeding flesh. Infinite air,
compressed from dizzy altitudes, now serves

his skullface as a pillow. Overhead
a vulture leers in solemn mockery,
knowing what John had never known: that dead
workers are dead before they cease to be.

— Edwin Rolfe

(Originally published as "The 100 Percenter" in the *Daily Worker*, 1928)

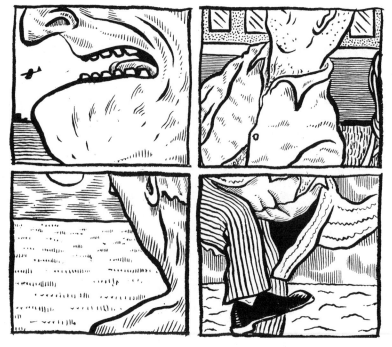

Russell Christian

Decatur, IL

JESSICA ABEL ©1997

AS OF TWO YEARS AGO, UNIONS CALLED DECATUR "THE WAR ZONE." THEY WERE IN CONFLICTS WITH THREE OF THE LARGEST EMPLOYERS THERE: ON STRIKE AT BRIDGESTONE/FIRESTONE AND CATERPILLAR, AND LOCKED OUT AT STALEY, A CORN-PROCESSING COMPANY. DAVE, GREG, AND I WENT TO DECATUR IN FEBRUARY TO SEE HOW THINGS HAD SORTED OUT.
— WHILE LOOKING FOR A PLACE TO GET A BITE TO EAT, WE STOP TO ADMIRE THE UNINTENTIONAL, BRUTAL BEAUTY OF THE INDUSTRIAL BRICOLAGE THAT IS THE STALEY PLANT, AND GET SO CARRIED AWAY THAT WE'RE SOON SNAPPING SOUVENIR PHOTOS OF THE RESTAURANT-THAT-USED-TO-BE-A-MR.-DONUT AND OF OURSELVES IN FRONT OF KREKEL'S KUSTARD--OUR CHOICE FOR LUNCH. A HELPFUL KREKEL'S EMPLOYEE SUGGESTS WE MIGHT FIND A WORTHIER PHOTO OP AT THE KREKEL'S JUST OUT OF TOWN, WHERE MR. KREKEL'S CHICKEN-CAR IS PARKED. WE DISAGREE. ANYWAY, WE HAVE OTHER PLANS.

OPEN ALL WINTER

Krekel's Kusto

I CONVINCE DAVE (WHO HAD MENTIONED THAT HE HAD INTENDED TO GET HIS HAIR CUT THAT MORNING, BUT OVERSLEPT) TO GET IT CUT AT A LITTLE BARBER-SHOP NEXT TO THE FAMILY DRUG AND THE FAMILY DOLLAR. BOTH HE AND GREG TAKE ON SOUTHERN ACCENTS FOR THE OCCASION. GREG CLAIMS HIS IS REAL, BUT I HAVE MY DOUBTS.

LABOR'S SETTLED DOWN A BIT AROUND HERE, FINALLY. THIS TOWN WAS DEVASTATED BY STALEY AND FIRESTONE.

I HAD A GUY WORKING FOR ME WHO HAD CROSSED HIS LINE. HE WAS NEAR RETIREMENT. A WORKER WHO WAS OUT CAME BY AND SAID TO ME, WHAT IS THAT GUY DOING HERE? AND I TOLD HIM HE WAS WORKING FOR ME. TWO OR THREE DAYS LATER, BUSINESS BOTTOMED OUT. THEY HAD POSTED A NOTICE IN THE UNION HALL. I HAD TO LET THE GUY GO. I SAID, HEY, THIS IS MY LIVELIHOOD. HE UNDERSTOOD.

LISA: THESE ARE PEOPLE WHO WANTED TO GET A JOB, GET MARRIED, BUY A HOUSE, HAVE KIDS, BUY A HARLEY, WHATEVER. THEY HIRED IN RIGHT OUT OF HIGH SCHOOL. THE UNION DIDN'T MEAN TOO MUCH, BUT THEN THERE'S THE CRISIS. BOOM -- 20, 25 YEARS LATER, ALL OF THE SUDDEN, EVERY-THING THEY HAD IS GONE. AND THEY FIND THEMSELVES RESEARCHING TAX DOCUMENTS ON THE COMPANY, AND GOING OFF ON SPEAKING TOURS, AND MEETING UP WITH NOAM CHOMSKY -- DOING STUFF THEY WOULD NEVER HAVE DONE IF IT HADN'T BEEN FOR THIS LOCKOUT.

ALL OF US WHO WENT OUT ON THE ROAD GOT AN EDUCATION ABOUT THE SOCIAL CLIMATE OF THIS COUNTRY. ABOUT UNDER-STANDING MINORITY RIGHTS AND ALTERNATIVE VIEWPOINTS -- SOCIALISTS, COMMUNISTS. THEY WEREN'T THE BOGEY MAN. I'M NOT A SOCIALIST, BUT A LOT OF WHAT THEY BELIEVE IS WHAT I BELIEVE.

MIKE GRIFFIN, HIRED IN TO STALEY IN 1966.

Solidarity

GOONZ 'N THE HOOD: UNION BUSTING

WOMEN'S

IN THE BATHROOM, NEXT TO THE TOILET, ALONG WITH THE HOUSE AND GARDEN MAGAZINES, THE WOMEN'S DAYS, I FOUND SOLIDARITY MAGAZINE.

WE'RE HUNGRY. PEOPLE KNOW--THE RANK AND FILE KNOWS WHAT STRUGGLE IS. MANY OF THEM HAVE BEEN THROUGH IT. THEY SEE AMERICA SLIPPING AWAY FROM THEM. SO THEY REACH OUT TO US TO HELP US.

PEOPLE WOULD TELL YOU: "I'M GIVING YOU THIS MONEY TO HELP YOU, BUT ALSO BECAUSE YOU'RE FIGHTING OUR FIGHT."

THERE WERE MOMENTS IN THE CONVERSATION WHEN I FELT LIKE ALL THIS TALK OF A GLOBAL ANTI-UNION CONSPIRACY SEEMED A LITTLE FAR-FETCHED. FASCINATING, BUT COULDN'T POSSIBLY BE TRUE, AT LEAST I HOPED NOT.

DETROIT-- THAT OUGHT TO BE OVER BY NEXT TUESDAY. RON CAREY OF THE TEAMSTERS IS GOING TO UNILATERALLY SURRENDER THAT STRUGGLE. IF THEY LOSE THAT TOWN, IT'S GOING TO BE THE SAME STORY IN EVERY CITY ACROSS AMERICA.

THE AMERICAN AIRLINES PILOTS ARE PREPARED TO GO OUT ON STRIKE. BUT IF BILL CLINTON ISSUES AN ORDER, THEY'LL OBEY THAT ORDER--AND IT'LL BE A BIG MISTAKE...

BUT IT TURNS OUT MIKE WAS RIGHT. A COUPLE DAYS AFTER OUR CONVERSATION, THE DETROIT NEWSPAPER UNIONS MADE AN OFFER TO RETURN TO WORK, AND THE PRESIDENT ORDERED THE PILOTS BACK TO WORK AFTER A TWO-MINUTE-LONG STRIKE, AND THEY WENT. THOUGH THESE GUYS ARE FREQUENTLY PORTRAYED AS A BUNCH OF DISGRUNTLED FORMER EMPLOYEES, HYSTERICAL AND UNRELIABLE, THEY TURN OUT TO KNOW BETTER THAN MOST OF US WHAT WE'RE UP AGAINST.

THE STALEY BUILDING, DECATUR, IL.

END. 4/4/97

Internment Camp

The Intern Economy and the Culture Trust
Jim Frederick

For a very brief period not too long ago I was the "chief of research" at a glossy yet rugged men's lifestyle magazine. An industry darling, this "practical guide to the sensory thrills and psychological rewards of an active physical life" (as its 1995 National Magazine Award write-up swooned), was one of the most celebrated and award-laden start-ups in recent memory. As they say in the industry, *Men's Journal* was "a very hot book."

Not coincidentally, it was also an advertiser's wet dream — a place where we took press releases at their word, where we re-shot photos for "personal grooming" stories because the toothbrushes didn't look "exciting" enough, and where being a "complete guide for high-performance living" (we used this phrase seriously) meant giving lavish coverage to every sexy consumer product we could get our comp-crazy hands on. In the pages of this morally bankrupt advertorial, this himbo of a magazine, you could, any given month, learn that speed-skiing was not only fun but fulfilling ("Courage wasn't what would propel me down Willamette. Innocence. I would become innocent."); read about the religious significance of mountain-biking equipment ("There's a Zen-like mystery about Giro's new Helios helmet."); be the first to know that this particular style of Nikes was much better than the one we said was the best ever a month ago (this one uses aircraft tubing!); and discover all the reasons why Howie Long is a really good actor.

But do not be impressed by the lofty title I held there. "Research chief" was pure euphemism for "the-fact-checker-whose-head-will-roll-if-anything-goes-wrong." In charge of the "legal invulnerability and factual accuracy" of the magazine, the bulk of my days involved determining whether octopi have pancreases (they don't), what the hell "aircraft tubing" actually is (nobody knows), and if ex-Oakland Raider wide receiver Warren Wells would sue us for calling him "compulsively felonious" (playing it safe, we ultimately cut the "compulsively" and never heard from him).

I was also partly in charge of finding interns to send our faxes, answer our phones, and, among other sundry responsibilities, go shopping for the products in photo shoots that we couldn't get comped. Compared to fact-checking, hiring interns was difficult stuff. Not because no one was willing, mind you. On the contrary, I was spoiled for choice. The applicants would walk in, these college kids, recent graduates, and grad students, always punctual and always white, sheepish but confident, polite, and well-fragranced. They would hand me clips from their school newspapers while I looked over their résumés, which always went something like this:

Interview Magazine
May '95 to Sept '95
Summer Intern

CBS News
Oct '94 to May '95
Fall Intern

The Village Voice
May '94 to August '94
Summer Intern

"Very impressive," I would say. By my quick calculations they had contributed,

conservatively, five or six thousand dollars worth of uncompensated work to various media conglomerates. I would tell them that they surely have all the "experience" they would ever get by following this strategy, and that while I had positions open (who doesn't have unpaid positions open?), I was reluctant to fill them with people who were already competent cub writers, reporters, editors, and fact-checkers. They should have been demanding jobs a long time ago. They would try not to look too crestfallen at this news. They would explain to me that they were indeed the perfect person to work for me for free. Hell, they sometimes said, they had been doing it so long that they were good at it by now.

Internships have never been more popular. According to the *New York Times*, the number of interns toiling for free has increased 30 percent in just three years, and internship guides, growing fatter every year, list anywhere between 50,000 to 100,000 positions. As tales of layoffs, "downsizing," and "right-sizing" (you only get one guess as to what that means) continue to flood the general business and mass market publications, internships are invariably presented as a refreshing bright spot of "opportunity" for the younger generation.

Don't worry that "cost controls and job cuts in the 1990s pushed many companies to shrink their training and recruiting departments," counsels an article in the December 4, 1996 *New York Times*. Big business is still looking out for you and "the surge in internships has created new opportunities for people like Jim Morabito," a guy who, it turns out,

held four internships before he even hit his senior year in college. While the vagaries of the information age visit hardship and ruination on families, towns, and entire regions, the intern economy is humming along unhindered, ballooning constantly, becoming an increasingly significant yet largely invisible segment of the American workforce. A study by Northwestern University determined that 26 percent of college graduates hired in 1993 had done some type of internship, compared to only 9 percent in 1992, and according to the author of the *Student's Guide to Volunteering*, volunteering alone comprises a $176 billion industry. Training may have been the paid beginning of your father's first job, but today you're supposed to get it on your own, often on your own tab.

With all the books, magazine articles, and pundits barraging us with an alarmingly unified rhetoric of, "Internships give you the edge in a competitive job market," "It's a win-win situation for both employer and intern," and "It's not a job, it's an education," it's easy to forget that internships are practically free money for big business. It's easy to forget that the kids are getting royally screwed.

Somewhere over the past two or three decades, a secret and shrewdly undeclared war between the titans of the glamour industries and a small undefended segment of the labor pool has been fought, and labor has lost. By deft public relations maneuvering, innovation in the face of decreasing cash flow, and the merciless leveraging of an ever-younger, starry-eyed, and unwary segment of the population, the media mandarins have cemented the institution of the internship — working for free — as not merely an acceptable route up the corporate ladder, but the expected one. Tomorrow's Mike Ovitzes, David Geffens, and Barry Dillers won't have started in the mailroom at William Morris, they will have been interns there.

IT'S safe to say that when 35 black sugar workers were shot dead while striking for a dollar a day in 1887 or when 500,000 Southern textile workers walked off the job in 1934, no one was thinking ahead to the summer of '96 when Jessica from Swarthmore would be sweating over the green glow of the Xerox machine, logging hundreds of unpaid hours as an MTV intern, assuring herself that this doesn't suck because now her CV will have "résumé radiance," as the authors of *America's Top Internships* like to put it. And granted, the intern class does not make a particularly sympathetic symbol of exploitation. It's hard to care about the plight of privileged college students when they themselves have volunteered for — demanded, even — this demeaning servitude. The inconvenient fact remains, however, that labor laws apply even to the rich, white, naive, and stupid (all necessary attributes for being an unpaid intern). And just because these hopeful careerists don't think of themselves as scabs, it doesn't mean they aren't.

There are almost as many definitions of "internship" these days as there are "internship programs" (over 100,000 by the Princeton Review's count). "Apprenticeships," as free-labor pundits such as Bob Weinstein, author of the formidably shameless *"I'll Work for Free!"*, call them, are as old as the Code of Hammurabi itself, suggesting a long and noble tradition of uncompensated tutelage in the workplace. (I often wonder if anyone will go the extra mile and assert that "interns" also built the pyramids, but they never do.) The Fair Labor Standards Act (FLSA) of 1938 — a typically meddlesome piece of federal legislation, in true Second Wave fashion — prohibited child labor, established a minimum wage for any kind of work within a for-profit institution, and stipulated that no one may work more than 40 hours a week without extra pay. The law was a major setback for employers of every stripe. For more than half a century, it forced the captains of industry (barring significant exceptions, of course) to cooperate with the newly established and accepted labor unions. A thoroughly blue-collar piece of legislation, the FLSA targeted only the most abusive employers of the time: factories, farms, and other heavy industries. It provided exemptions for charities, churches, and other perpetually cash-strapped non-profit organizations who had always (and still do) filled their ranks with young volunteers.

There is, however, another exemption in the FLSA. Vaguely worded, it concerns "trainees," or the oddly redundant "student learners." It allows for-profit institutions to pay short-term employees less than the minimum wage if they are there in an educational capacity. The Department of Labor requires that six criteria be met before it considers someone not an "employee" but a "trainee" exempt from the FLSA: The training is similar to that one would get in school; the training is for the benefit of the trainees, not the employer; the trainees do not displace regular workers; the employer derives no immediate advantage from the activities of the trainees, and may even incur some loss; the trainees understand that they are not entitled to a job at the conclusion of the training; and the trainees understand that they are not entitled to wages for the time spent in training.

Even though the Department of Labor doesn't use or even recognize the word "intern," this clearly

legitimate educational arrangement is what certain branches of industry — banks, law firms, tech companies, engineering companies, and many federal agencies — refer to when they use the term. College students follow a highly structured path of seminars, lectures, on-the-job training, personal "mentors," and company-assigned moot projects. And, despite the exemption, many of these interns are still quite well-paid.

The real abusers of the intern economy, however, are the glamour industries. Fashion, architecture, and virtually every media outlet (except for newspapers and some magazines, with their fuss-budgety unions) piggy-back on the credibility of the more legitimate programs by hiring college kids as little more than clerical temps, paying them not a dime, and disguising the whole operation as a "learning experience." It is not a coincidence that the industries offering youngsters an unending parade of subversive cartoons, daring advertising, and rebellious photo spreads are also the ones most likely to strip their earning power from them. It's almost their duty, as the institutions that have taught us to value style over substance, to take advantage of people's resulting faith that working someplace cool is better than getting a paycheck.

But why should the rest of us care if Chip from Brown, who fetches coffee for the green-room guests, is an "intern," not a "temp"? Or if the entire student bodies of Mt. Holyoke, Amherst, Columbia, and Vassar are stupid enough to sign away their summers to Wenner and Eisner, Geffen and Redstone?

First, a bit of basic employment-market economics. The glamour industries enjoy a tremendous surplus of labor. There are more people who want media jobs than can be employed. Therefore labor is cheap, as demonstrated by the industry's already low salaries ($18,000 a year for an editorial assistant is not uncommon, which is about $9 dollars an hour, assuming the most optimistic work schedule possible). Left to its own devices, a rational market with surplus labor will bid wages down almost to the point where no one will accept a job. If it can, a market will bid the wages all the way down to zero, as long as someone, anyone, will do the work, for whatever real or imagined benefit. Which brings us back to Jessica and Chip. For them and their classmates the imagined benefits of an internship are so great that real benefits — you know, wages — have been bid out of existence. Businesses, obviously, have a real, bottom-line incentive to encourage the trend toward labor that is not only free, but without any type of obligation whatsoever. In other words, interns are restructuring the labor market. Thanks to those who can afford to win the labor auction with the lowest possible price — *I'll work for free!* — those without outside (read "parental") support are forced to take tremendous real-dollar losses to stay competitive, or they are simply priced out of competition entirely. This ensures that the glamour industries remain the land of the rich and privileged, for they are the only people who can absorb a short-term loss to get an imagined long-term gain.

But why stop there? Left unchecked, a labor market knows no boundaries when it comes to exploitation. Although the intern price floor can't go any lower dollar-wise, it can go lower by the amount of time served, or by the size of the labor segment drawn into the swindle. As more people do internships, the supply of intern-alums increases, driving the value of that "experience" down even further — a phenomenon you could call "intern inflation." So college kids feel pressure to do more of them, or for a longer stretch of time. And those previously thought of as obvious employee potential, like college graduates, grad students, and career-changers, are increasingly told, "Have you thought of doing an internship?"

Without some sort of check, this admirably efficient market will just continue on its merry way. Not long from now we will begin hearing: "Summer internships don't really give you that much experience because they are only 12 weeks long. You need at least a semester or even a year to get a real grounding." It is not outlandish to imagine a day when a year's internship is explicitly required before you get hired for a new job, or when employers start charging interns for, let's say, "training costs." Before we laugh at Jessica and Chip for exploiting themselves, we should consider that years of Jessicas and Chips have already made unpaid internships for certain jobs an unspoken requirement, and the longer the intern economy hums along unhindered, the more this labor inflation will increase. By giving away work, interns reduce the value of everybody's labor.

How much have they cheapened our lives? Since statistics concerning interns aren't counted by the Department of Labor, it's nearly impossible to estimate. But the figures for individual intern-exploiters are readily available. Take MTV, which alone uses between 150 and 200 interns at any given time and requires from each at least two days a week of work. There are three seasons — summer, fall, and spring. A 12-week summer intern is forfeiting $989 if he works the minimum two days a week; $2,472 if full time. A 20-week spring and fall intern gives up $1,648 if he works two-day weeks; $4,120 for full time. How does MTV make out in all this? Very well, thanks. Granting MTV the minimums for all variables of its program (150 interns working only two days a week),

MTV saves $642,270 a year in unpaid wages. To extend these calculations nationwide, assume there are 40,000 internships every year (the low end of the internship guides' estimates) and they all work only two days a week for only 12 weeks (again, all low-end estimates). What do you get? Every year kids forfeit and businesses gain more than $39,522,000.

And that's not all internships do. Take a trip to any design studio, advertising agency, or editorial office (even the most responsible left-wing publications) and you'll see one of the glamour industries' dirtiest secrets: There's not a black face in the joint. If you can't get a job unless you've had an internship, and you can't take an internship unless you can be supported by daddy for a couple months, then the system guarantees an applicant pool that is decidedly privileged. But you needn't let a little arithmetic and your innate sense of decency bother you. Do what the free-labor advocates have been doing for years now: Simply holler, "Internships are not racist and elitist!" as loud as you can; repeat as necessary until you believe it.

To be sure, these are tough times for workers in media-land. Newspaper firings aren't even news anymore; networks are cutting back on personnel in every department; meanwhile, tabloid and TV talk shows, with their low overhead and small staffs, continue to draw huge audiences. Indeed, the only asset that many media outlets have left is their cultural cachet, their name brand appeal, the fact that they are cool. As the job market tightens and the ratio of college graduates to total employable adults increases, there is an ever-increasing glut of "marketing" and "communications" majors who will work for free.

Unhindered by the regulatory watchdogs that continue to plague sweatshops, factories, and farms, the media-market is only too happy to oblige them. Those MBAs who now rule the newsrooms are no fools, after all.

Vernon Stone, a professor of journalism at the University of Missouri, and one of the few researchers who has acknowledged the downside of unpaid media internships through the years, notes, "Unpaid internships, once rolling, tended to crowd the paid ones off the road. In 1976, 57 percent of the TV and 81 percent of the radio stations with interns paid at least some of them. By 1991, only 21 percent of the TV and 32 percent of the radio stations with interns were paying....Seven times as many [unpaid interns] were in TV newsrooms in 1991 as in 1976. Radio's increase was fivefold."

Stone cautions that every employer should make sure they comply with the law, but the.chances that any company would actually be held responsible for labor violations are miniscule. The only time a company has been nailed for intern abuse in recent memory was in March 1995, when A. Brown-Olmstead Associates, an Atlanta public relations firm, was ordered to pay back wages of $31,520 to 42 interns. The problem was not that they failed the Labor Department's "immediate advantage" test of "trainee" labor — hell, almost everybody would fail that one. The clincher was that they had the audacity to bill their clients for the interns' work, thereby putting an exact dollar amount on the toil they weren't compensating.

All Internships Lead to MTV

Given the fact that they benefit so handsomely from the intern economy, it is no surprise that the media routinely run stories on the virtues of internships. The stories always seem to follow the same pattern. First comes the bad news about how tough it is out there: "For 17 years straight, A. Todd Iannucelli made a late summer trip to the stationery store to buy loose-leaf sheets for classroom note-taking," goes one cautionary tale that appeared in August 1995 in the *Washington Post*. "This year, he went to replenish a dwindling supply of résumé paper, having joined a growing number of college grads who, as fall approaches, remain jobless and planless." Then they assure us that internships are the only way a college kid is going to get by in the cutthroat world of the Culture Trust: "Consultants say the route has become a popular one with savvy jobseekers," the *Post* continues. "For a new entrant into the job market, volunteering or unpaid internships may be the only ways to amass credentials."

It should hardly surprise us, given the amount they stand to gain from the unfettered operating of the intern economy, that the hippest publications are among the most regular and most sanguine chroniclers of the intern's happy lot. *Rolling Stone*, a notorious intern abuser, runs gooey features on the glories of unpaid internships in its annual college issue. One year it profiled the lucky guy who drove the Oscar Meyer weinermobile, the even luckier guy who got to fetch lunch for Howard Stern, and, luckiest of all, the New York Knicks towel guy. But *Rolling Stone* doesn't want Chip and Jessica getting swollen heads just because they get to sweat for the stars, and so on occasion it will tincture the standard categories of the intern story with a certain wholesome contempt for the young people who so put themselves out for the glamour business. "You would be surprised how many intelligent people cannot take a cohesive phone message or Xerox more than one copy of a document," it quoted Victoria Rowan, a woman who had risen from internhood to be a powerful and glamorous assistant editor at *Mirabella*, as saying back in 1993. "It's not a game of shit on the peon. Coffee has to be ordered." Indeed it does, gentle Victoria. But if you're not paying the peon minimum you are, in fact, shitting on her. Even girl-empowering *Sassy* gets in on the act, following in 1995 the heroic exploits of an intern at — surprise — MTV: "Biggest perk: We got to go to Madonna's Bedtime Story Pajama Party at Webster Hall (a huge club in New York City). Worst part of the job: We have to go up to the 50th floor a lot, and the elevator makes me nauseous."

But to read the most addle-eyed intern-economy glorification of all you have to turn to the new *New Yorker*, which in October 1994 ran "Rocking in Shangri-La," a story by John Seabrook about interns at — you guessed it — MTV. The story actually attempts to convince readers that "the real power brokers" at MTV are not President Shirley McGrath, Chair Tom Freston, or even Viacom Chair Sumner Redstone, but its "employees under the age of twenty-five." "When you are in your early twenties and you are working for MTV," Seabrook writes, in one of the most appallingly misguided tributes to the Culture Trust to appear to date, "you carry in your brain, muscles, and gonads a kind of mystical authority that your bosses don't possess." After 14 long pages it turns out that the "authority" possessed by the low-paid production assistants and the unpaid interns boils down to this: They are walking, talking demographic surveys who tell executives what is cool and what sucks. In exchange, they get free MTV stuff! And they're allowed to listen to music as loud as they want! Often, observes the venerable *New Yorker*, interns will "rock out together for a moment before continuing along the hall," because, we are told, "employees who think that a particular song 'rules' are encouraged to crank it."

IT is nearly impossible to raise a battle cry for a war that has already been lost. Knowing too well that old notions like government protection for the exploited, fair wages, and — not to sound quaint — common decency will probably never catch up with the go-go information age, the Culture Trust has won this battle even before the other combatants had realized it started. The tide of indentured college servitude is unstoppable and the market for free labor can only get worse in the near future.

Don't bother looking to government. The people who passed the FLSA have long since been supplanted by the likes of Ohio Republican Rep. Joe Knollenberg, who fights courageously to liberate *employers* from the tyranny of paying a fair day's wage for a fair day's work. In January, Knollenberg introduced an amendment to the FLSA entitled the "Job Skills Development Act of 1997," which aims to revoke the basic provision that labor contributing to the wealth of someone else must be compensated. When he introduced a virtually identical bill in 1995, Knollenberg told the House Subcommittee on Workforce Protections that the FLSA "places an unnecessary burden on individuals seeking employment in a competitive profession ... Frankly, the FLSA restrictions on volunteer services illustrate why the American people believe their

federal government is too intrusive." What Knollenberg doesn't mention is that without that "intrusiveness," any sweatshop proprietor or factory foreman could legally claim that the work their scabs are doing is "volunteer work" aimed at "furthering their career goals." After all, they're only trainees at the drill bit, learning skills that will help them get ahead in a competitive job market.

Curiously enough, there have been some hopeful developments in fields where the would-be exploiters of interns are bound by a professional code of ethics. The American Institute of Architects (AIA) instituted a program a few years ago to combat unfair labor practices by its members. Every architect who receives an award from the AIA or makes a speech at its meetings must sign a document affirming that his or her company upholds all tenets of the FLSA and the association's agreed-upon labor practices. But this is an anomaly permitted by the unique position of the AIA within its industry. Any hope that the National Association of Broadcasters, the Council of Fashion Designers of America, and the Academy of Motion Pictures Arts and Sciences would follow suit is almost laughable.

As for the interns themselves, it would be a little naive to imagine that the children of the white-collar class could make some stand of solidarity and resist, at any and all times, working for free. The era is simply too selfish, EMI Records too alluring, MTV too sexy, *Spin* too hip, Frank Gehry too prestigious, and CBS too powerful. The glamour titans will have all the free labor they will ever need. And in a world where we are forced to mortgage pieces of our soul every day, we are increasingly going to have to give it away for free.

My Dad Went to San Quentin and All I Got Was This Lousy T-Shirt

Christian Parenti

BOB TESSLER is just your average entrepreneur, out looking for that little something that makes the whole system tick: people who will work hard and make him rich. To "stay ahead of the competitors," Bob needs workers who won't talk back, take sick days, have babies, or make personal calls on company time. Where is a guy like Bob gonna find such good old-fashioned values? He tried Mexico, but the "corruption" was a big hassle. He could go to Malaysia, but that's too far away, and too expensive for Bob's little "literature assembly" and "data retrieval" firm called DPAS. Plus, Bob's a hip guy; he cares; he wants to give back. So Bob opened shop in California's oldest maximum security prison — San Quentin, a.k.a. La Pinta.

"We have a captive labor force," says Bob innocently. "The whole thing is very profitable." You bet it is! Plus the rent is almost free and Bob gets a fat tax break for being so socially responsible and hiring cons. There's another reason DPAS — which enjoys such illustrious clients as Chevron, Macy's and Bank Of America — closed its information age maquiladora in Tecate, Mexico and came back home in '92: flexibility. It's the magic word these days. With "globalization" and that "space-time compression," flexibility — that is, the freedom to fire and hire workers at will — is what business in the Nineties is all about.

"Now we can make minute changes in an order on the drop of a dime," Bob exults. And, hey, that pleases the customers too! True, wages of $4.25 an hour (80 percent of which goes to the state), are higher in a U.S. prison than in Mexico, but overall the costs of production are lower and profits larger. By the way, Bob's new work force doesn't have the right to organize a union, strike, give interviews to the media (thanks to a recent crackdown by California's governor) and has extremely limited access to community groups and other potential troublemakers. Bob's not the only one helping out the low-lifes at San Quentin. There's also the ironic entrant, an apparel firm called "Inkarcerated," which makes exercise clothes, emblazoned with slogans like "My Dad Went to San Quentin and All I Got Was This Lousy T-Shirt" and "Fitness is a Life Sentence." If there's a mistake in the printing, they just stamp "Parole Denied" on the item and ship it out anyway!

The only thing preventing DPAS and Inkarcerated from using even more labor at San Quentin is the massive wave of incarceration itself. Due to the ever more radical round-up of California's poor, San Quentin has been transformed from a regular prison into Northern California's carceral induction center. Thus, most San Quentin prisoners are "just passing through" on their way to some other, brand new island in the state's far flung concrete archipelago.

But elsewhere there are plenty of convicts staying put for a very long time, and plenty of state legislators willing to serve 'em up like buckets of fish to the best-connected bidder. California, Nevada, Oregon, and Washington lead the nation in leasing prison labor to private firms. In Nevada, prisoners already make waterbeds for Vinyl Products; restore cars for Imperial Palace; hand-assemble $500,000 Shelby Cobra road cars; build stretch limousines for Emerald Coach; and manufacture Bentley Nevada circuit boards for nuclear power plants. In Washington state, an article in *The Stranger* reports, a company called Exmark uses a "flexible" pool of prison laborers to package cool stuff ranging from Microsoft Windows 95 to Starbucks Coffee products to JanSport gear, and literature for telecommunications giant US WEST (which has recently cornered the market on prisoner calling cards — small world). In Vermont, prisoners book holiday reservations, as do their counterparts in Wisconsin, where prisoners were briefly used in nocturnal shelf-stocking at Toys R Us.

In Arizona, even the 109 residents of death row are now pulling their own weight on a prison-run vegetable farm. One of the positive side-effects of employing the condemned — as far as the governor's press secretary is concerned — is that the inmates will now be too busy to file "frivolous lawsuits in attempts to circumvent their death sentences."

The benefits to guys like Bob are even more obvious. During a strike by TWA flight attendants in the late 1980s, the ever-conscientious California Youth Authority helped soothe the labor dispute by providing inmates as TWA tickets bookers. The extra capacity allowed TWA to transfer ticket agents to flight attendant positions. According to one union official "this very definitely allowed the airline latitude in replacing strikers." In other words, the state helped put those rebellious sky-bunnies back in their place.

The wonderful thing about prison labor is that its impact reverberates far beyond the prison gates. If prisoners will do data entry for Third World wages, why should an employer hire some

slacker temp for 13 bucks an hour? And if the employer does decide to take the slacker temp route, why should they let the irritating bastard go to the bathroom whenever he wants when there is a labor force as well-behaved as prisoners just outside town? By making even the worst job seem like a gift, prison labor promises to put a smile on everyone's face.

Some will say that the reappearance of prison labor reminds them a little too much of the 19th century South. Others, usually politically illiterate leftists, shriek: "The return of slavery!" But the fact of the matter is that prison labor is better than slavery. You can't fire a slave, but when you no longer need an inmate's services — hey, it's back to the hole, as easy as that. Also, the state wouldn't feed, clothe, house, or discipline your slave. But they will do all that for your inmate temp. It's more like slavery lite — all the work with only half the overhead.

Besides, prison labor was never the enemy of progress that its opponents portray. Even in the post-Civil War "New South," the heyday of convict leasing, Southern prison labor was not about saving the antebellum plantation economy. Instead, as Alex Lichtenstein has shown in *Twice the Work of Free Labor*, the vast majority (and politically most important segment) of convict labor was used to catapult Southern heavy industry from stagnant shallows of post-war disarray to fully modernized profitability. In Georgia, for example, more than 80 percent of leased convicts (and all but the very ill were leased) worked in factories, mines, and railroads. Only 14 percent or less did plantation work. In other words, convicts did not replace slaves.

What convicts did do was provide 19th-century Bobs with a very well behaved, shock-troop proletariat at a time of terrible social upheaval and labor unrest. Convicts built the South's railroads, mined its coal, made its steel, graded its roads, and turned its pine barrens into turpentine. The clock-punching work culture of these modern industries was difficult for former farmers and agricultural slaves to get used to. So it really helped having guards and armed "trusties" there to, well, kill malingerers. If the state and its gun-toting invigilators hadn't been there to bull-whip and beat convicts, the South might never have "passed the test" and graduated to full-fledged industrial capitalism.

It's no coincidence that those were also the years of the worst union troublemaking in our history. Convicts were Southern entrepreneurs' preferred strikebreakers and were often used to lock out pugnacious workers. This helped keep wages low, at about the one bowl of lard-flavored mash a day level. Of course it also infuriated a lot of people. On several occasions, the United Mine Workers attacked convict labor camps, and kept the imprisoned scabs out of the

pits by force. During one strike in Tennessee, the UMW overran a convict camp, burned it to the ground, and set all the inmates loose (a problem we don't have today, thanks to somnambulant unions and prisons surrounded by the new high-voltage electrical "death fence").

Southern inmate labor also had wide-ranging, shall we say, "cultural influences." While it's true most convicts worked in factories and mines, the plantation system wasn't entirely out of the picture. With the end of slavery, planters were faced with a huge problem — how to keep down the local majority, that is, the black people. Enter the racialized discourse of "black crime." As soon as the Civil War was over, white Southerners went on a massive lock-up spree and 80 to 90 percent of the new prisoners were black. The new post-slavery judicial system served a dual purpose: It rounded up willing hands for the emerging industrial sector and at the same time intimidated rural African-Americans back into "traditional" social relations of "deference." It was a win-win thing, Southern style.

Why does all this sound so familiar here at the *fin* of another *siècle*? If we discount numerology, we're left with only political and economic explanations. Once again the state has embarked on a racist incarceration binge and begun subsidizing capital with prison labor. And — surprise! Once again the economy is undergoing a massive restruct-uring, in the aftermath of a traumatic crisis. Then it was the de-vastation of a nasty civil war and the shift to an industrial capitalist economy; today's crisis was the 1970s nightmare of falling pro-fitability, stagnant growth, in-flation and intense international competition. Remember the OPEC price shocks of '73 and '79, the Sandinista revolution, all those post-Vietnam wildcat strikes? That stuff made life hard for entrepreneurs like Bob.

Reagan's and Clinton's rollback of America's welfare state (granted, it was puny but it was big enough to give people ideas) was part of the answer, as was a serious ass-kicking for the Third World. But an ever-more disciplined domestic workforce with lower expectations is also crucial. There's a lot of competition out there. Wages in Haiti and Honduras are

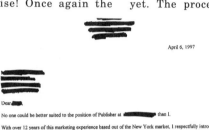

April 6, 1997

Dear ▆▆▆

No one could be better suited to the position of Publisher at ▆▆▆▆▆▆ than I.

With over 12 years of this marketing experience based out of the New York market, I respectfully introduce myself to you as a means to add the "heaviest" of "heavy hitters" to head up your team of sales and marketing professionals.

My publishing experience ranges from new product development to project implementation, inclusive of the marketing positioning, strategy and proposal/presentation (inclusive of financials) development and creation, as well as, comprehensive sales responsibilities.

I have created and sold magazine/newspaper concepts, hardcover/softcover book programs, promotions, sales positioning proposals and media kits, amongst many other "intangible" marketing tools (namely advertising).

I am a conceptual wizard with the marketing strengths, vision, and intelligence to bring ideas I conceive of in the shower to fruition!

I am an "Out-of-the-Box Thinker" and have had great success in new business development and management of millions of dollars in the corporate publishing environment by taking the time to understand my prospective clients. I have even provided sales training and motivational seminars for my clients' sales staffs to excite and incent them internally about the programs I was selling-in at the top!

I would very much appreciate the opportunity to talk to you about how my new business and strategic development skills and *team management philosophy* would fit to the achievements and visions you have for ▆▆▆▆▆ growth and future.

I hope you enjoy the enclosed writing samples, both of which I feel fairly represent my thought process and method of management.

I will make a list of updated personal references available to you upon a personal interview.

Thank you, in advance, for your consideration.

Sincerely, ▆▆▆

so low you need a microscope to count 'em. But try telling that to workers back at home. That's the reason guys like Bob and feisty startups like Inkarcerated need a little help from the state. Presto, prison labor, working its market magic at the thin edge of the wedge in emerging industries like software production, literature assembly, telemarketing, and exercise apparel.

And it's not like the changes are over yet. The process of restructuring continues with the repeal of welfare, NAFTA, and the 1996 election's coddling of big business. There's going to be another blizzard of pink-slips before we get this all worked out. All of which is eventually — let's face it — going to make a lot of people uppity. Criminal justice can help to solve the problem, re-gulating both bodies and prices: You get the unemployed white guys to guard the unemployed African-American and Latino guys. And the really lucky member of both groups get to star in reruns of *Cops* and *American Prison Guard*.

Convict labor is not archaic, but cutting edge; not incongruous with "the free market," but capitalism's tool of choice. And guys like Bob are leading the way. They aren't just making gadgets, they're making a bright new future for all of us. A future free of whining unions and spoiled workers; a future of diligence, punctuality, gratitude. A future with a smart-ass "Parole Denied" stamped on its face.

One Thing About a Goat
Lydia Millet

ANIMALS don't have it so good. It's no secret. One thing's clothes: you won't see a goat browsing in Petites on Saturday afternoon. You won't see a goat exercising her rights as a consumer. I'm not saying they can help it, I'm just saying it bugs me. I mean it just bothers me, when I see a goat. Maybe three times I've seen a goat, and every time I'm going: What does this goat have to offer me personally? Another thing, a goat's no big drinker. Friday comes around, a goat can just not celebrate. What does a goat do when he's bored? Nothing, that's the answer. Nothing. I'm talking this goat has no hobbies. Appreciation of music? You can forget it.

I'm not a goat-hater or anything. When I say goat, I could mean giraffe, I could mean trout. Sure, they look different. I know that. But as far as I can tell they're basically the same. In terms of conversation, for instance. You see an animal, you go yep, there's an animal. That's as far as it goes. There are things you can do, sure. You can feed it, touch it, or kill it. That's basically it. I don't know. It just bugs me.

Stairmaster always makes me think. Since that crappy Discman broke I'm stepping, stepping and thinking like there's no tomorrow. I get home after my workout and my brain is more exhausted than my hamstrings. The problem is whether to send it to the manufacturer or buy a new one, either way you're getting ripped off. That right there is another thing. A goat wouldn't have a clue about that. Sixty- or 90-day warranty? A goat doesn't give a shit. I mean I know they don't buy stuff but say they did. I mean, what is that? I can't figure it out. It's actually making me mad at this moment. Show me a goat right

now, I'll shake him till his teeth fall out.

Screaming won't do you any good though, with a goat. If I had ESP I would read the mind of a goat. It would probably look like ASCII. 0s and 1s. Okay so I don't know what ASCII looks like. Big deal. There's Mister Computer Guy Chris sitting on my shoulder like an organ grinder's monkey. There's a guy who pretends to know everything. He may be smart but ask him what a goat's long-term goals are, he'll be stymied too. It doesn't stop him from lording it over me. I can get some guy's mortgage schedule from Akron, that's what he says. You got any old friends in Shreveport? he asks. Gimme their names, I'll tell you if they're rich or poor. I show him I'm not impressed. All it takes is a shrug. Uh huh Chris, I go, and return to my transaction. He slouches away like an old hunchback.

The worst is when he tells his theories. You're on break drinking a Coke and he corners you in the employee lounge, eating from his ziploc bag of dry Cheerios. He says It's all chains. Nothing is separate. He says This is the era of mergers. He says By the time we're retired there won't be such a thing as the U. S. of A., it'll be owned by Time Warner. He goes Every time you pay with your credit card people know all about you. They track everything you buy. They can describe you like they've known you all your life. You ever had an appendectomy? Well they know it. Luckily I can deal with him now. At first I was polite but then I learned. For instance yesterday when he was theorizing I crushed my can, lobbed it into the trash and walked out the lounge door. It shut him right up. I know this because once I turned the corner I stayed there for a second and heard his sentence trail off. It's not worth it. There comes a point when being polite is the same as stabbing a fork in your arm.

Stay on track. Animal thoughts. I like to take one thought and follow through, when I'm on the Stairmaster. To see if I can do it. It's harder than I expected. There's an obese woman stepping next to me. You just want to lean over and say honey, give up. Go home and scarf some lard. Shove your face in a lard cake and gobble. It won't make a difference. It reminds me of one positive thing about goats, which is also a negative. They don't have opinions. They're pretty much neutral, as far as I know. For instance politics. There's no goat out there lobbying for animal rights in Washington D.C. Sure, I know it's obvious but what do they do all day? I'm not talking about grazing or leaping. I mean what do they want? Nothing, that's the answer. A goat's problem is it has no desires. Okay, needs. It needs a hunk of grass, for instance. That's what makes a goat boring. It doesn't want zip. Nothing. The big bagel.

Mister Computer is boring too and that's gotta be why. He doesn't strive, he has no ambition. He just fiddles. Fiddles, brags, and tells his theories. He's steady-state, like a goat. Entropy increases. A law of thermal dynamics like on Discovery Channel. Mister Computer never heard of the Big Bang. All he knows about is finding out the status of a car loan in Salt Lake City. He just wants to go on like he's going.

She's got a Discman but it's just a matter of time. Give up physical fitness lady, and I'll be taking that Discman. I'm reading the cards and I see heart disease in your future. You won't need the Discman anymore. It'll break on the ninety-first day anyway. Jesus she's even sporting a *Vogue* magazine T-shirt. It's like a paraplegic guy wearing ski boots. Hope's fine and all but please there are limits. You have to see what's realistic.

A goat doesn't plan for the future. If there were IRAs for goats they wouldn't get many takers. 401(k) for goats? I don't think so.

Then there was the trip to Vermont in the Cressida when we got out to see a view and there was a goat at the fence. It was dirtier than your petting-zoo goats but that wasn't what got to me. What got to me was how this goat stood there without doing anything, not even eating. Maybe it was sick, but it threw me for a loop. I remember I looked at the goat and there was no expression there. That goat had no facial expression. You don't expect them to smile I mean that could be disturbing, but this goat had blank eyes. Maybe it was sick. Or deficient. A retard goat. Hard to tell the difference. You could break down and sob right there and it would have no response. They're not supportive. You could die right there, you could expire at the feet of that goat and then what would happen? Nothing is what. The goat wouldn't notice. I don't know, there's something about that.

There she goes. That six minutes really took it out of her. Her butt moves in a rotary swing. Another rotisserie chicken flaps up and takes her place. She's looking at me for longer than normal. Twenty Minute Limit When Others Are Waiting I'm sure. The race is to the swift, hogface.

Mister Computer has a dog. It's small and ugly. It has a skin condition that makes its hair fall out. Don't even talk to me about halitosis, that dog has breath that could fell a man at ten paces. He brought it into the office one morning and hid it under his desk in a box. What does he think, the dog loves him for who he is? You can like pets a lot until you notice they can't tell the difference between you and anyone else. No judgment and no values. The proof is in the pudding. That dog followed Mister Genius around like he was Jesus Christ Our Lord. Why, because he wanted food. Zero discrimination. You can't take a dog aside and tell him his owner is a loser. Not receptive. Goats are the same except they don't follow anyone. They eat off the ground, not out of a bowl. That's all it is.

No, excuse *me*. Instead of standing in line why doesn't she make hay while the sun shines and use the Nautilus? This is the land of opportunity, correct me if I'm wrong.

Stay on track. That always happens when I'm having a thought, someone interrupts it or something distracts me. It could be a minor incident but it breaks the thread and then you have to start all over again. You fall into the chinks of the thought and can't get back out. It's a major problem with thoughts in general. There should be rooms just for thinking with signs up saying Do Not Disturb. No one would go there though. I probably wouldn't either. You don't limit yourself to one activity at a time, you wouldn't be able to fit them all in.

Goat goat goat. It's a good question whether, if you were locked in the same house with one particular goat for thirty years, you'd ever come to an understanding. For instance if you were jailed with a goat for a cellmate. Sure you'd get used to the goat and you could predict how it was going to act, but that's different. There's scientists that teach chimpanzees to talk in sign language. Okay fine goats don't have hands, but maybe they have other talents and are just very quiet. You never know that about an animal. It's frustrating. Some guys are that way too. Not Mister Computer. They could cut off his tongue and he'd keep right on telling theories, with charades or cue cards or something. You can't be a fly on the wall of a goat brain.

What bugs me is how he could think he had a right to say it. Like he's anyone to say anything. No one pays attention to him, no one. No one ever agrees with him. If you took a poll it's a good bet most people would rate him 0 on a 1 to 10 scale. 2 or 3 tops. Ginette in Customer

Service laughs when he says stuff, she might give him a 3. That's the best he would do. Ginette likes people, that's what she said in her interview. She goes I'm a people person. Real original Ginette. Her 3 would be his highest rating, and she'd probably give Adolf Hitler a 3 too. She likes people. You could say, But Ginette he committed mass genocide, and she'd go, Well it was probably out of insecurity. She says that whenever someone acts like an asshole. He's just insecure, she goes. Yeah Ginette. She'd be good to have along if your plane crashed in the Himalayas and you had nothing to eat, like that movie. She'd tear chunks of flesh off her own body and sauté it on the wing to feed the injured crew. She'd be walking around with missing body parts smiling like an idiot. You could go Ginette you look a lot worse without your left thigh. She'd giggle and say Chill girl, you aready hungry agin?

Anyway even if he really thinks it he shouldn't have said it. There's such a thing as a good workplace attitude. You don't just say what you think.

Now she's flapping off again and offering her Stairmaster to the next person in line extremely loudly while shooting a look at me. It's like sorry, but I have needs. Mister Chris may ignore them, that doesn't mean they're not there. Was I doing anything wrong? No, is the answer. I was minding my own business in the lounge. I was trying to read *People* which I don't see what's wrong with that. There's nothing wrong with trying to have a little time to yourself when you're on break. There's nothing wrong with wanting to know what's going on in the world. Maybe he should try reading more often himself. As usual he walks in slumping and snacking and trying to tell me the future. The future according to Mister Computer. I go We don't want to hear it. That's all I said. He's a windbag. No one appreciates that. No one else would say anything, they're too weak. Then I went back to *People*.

Four minutes to go and if they think I'm stopping one minute early they can give it up. Forty-five minutes nonstop is my rule. They've been distracting me the whole time, that should be enough for them. I could say Are you happy? I lost my chain of thought because of you and what did that even accomplish? People like you are the ones who stop all half-decent thoughts from coming to bloom. It's no wonder the world is confused and has problems, it's pushy people like you. Goat goat goat. See? It gets me nowhere now. The whole thing was a waste.

He leaned down with his hand on the arm of the couch and put his face up close to mine. Too close for comfort. He and his dog have more in common than psoriasis I'll say that much. He said You know what? Shut your mouth. Just shut up. You're a teller. You're just a stupid teller.

INDUSTRIAL HOSPITALITY—*in the South*

Unions Can't Buy Elections, But Let's Pretend They Can

Rob Boatright

IT was late October 1996, and Congressman Frank Cremeans was in trouble. Polls showed the Republican freshman running neck-and-neck in Ohio's Sixth Congressional District with the man he narrowly unseated in 1994, Democrat Ted Strickland. Republican Majority Leader Dick Armey showed up on October 30 and lent Cremeans a hand by stumping throughout his poor, Appalachian district. Armey implored the voters not to be fooled by the "voter education guides" that the AFL-CIO had been airing on local television stations. The Sixth, despite its large contingent of steelworkers and brick plant workers, would be, according to Armey, a district where "big labor" was taught a lesson. "We want to win at a level that would humiliate them!" he told one crowd.

Cremeans lost the election by 2.4 percentage points, or 5,300 votes. Did the AFL-CIO's campaign make the difference here? Maybe. But if anyone in the district really wanted to get the dirt on Cremeans, they could have found it just about anywhere: The *Dayton Daily News* anointed Cremeans' 1994 candidacy a "bad joke," and a number of southern Ohio newspapers carried news of Cremeans' nomination by *The Progressive* as one of the ten "dimmest bulbs" in Congress. During the campaign, Cremeans made odd insinuations about the sexual abilities of his opponent and declared that homosexuality had caused the fall of the Roman Empire. In 1996, he accused Strickland of being anti-Christian, of abetting riots in the Lucasville State Penitentiary, and of stealing machinery from Cremeans' concrete mixing business. It's hard to say that anyone who cared about the election enough to pay attention to the AFL-CIO commercials didn't already have plenty of reasons to vote against Cremeans.

But let's say that labor did make the difference, as both the AFL-CIO and Cremeans have claimed. In fact, let's suppose, just for the sake of argument, that labor money made the difference in each of the 19 races in which incumbent Republicans were defeated. What then? Well, if you listen to much of the news media, it means that labor is in big trouble. Linda Killian, writing in *The New Republic*, claims that "What the AFL-CIO may have bought is a GOP majority that will do everything it can to ensure that labor pays for its ambitions." Republican National Committee Chair Haley Barbour has vowed that campaign finance will be reformed to curb the baleful influence of labor. Laughable though the prospects of campaign finance reform may seem, labor's $35 million campaign got plenty of people mad enough to talk about it. Republicans have pledged to attack labor on a number of fronts — to curtail the ability of unions to use membership dues for campaign advocacy, to make it more difficult for workers to get overtime pay, and to allow companies to reduce unions' bargaining power by setting up company unions.

Today, after six months of revelations about corporate donors and the corruption their money spawned, labor's contributions seem both clean and remarkably puny. What was all the fuss about? Only 19 of the 64 incumbent Republicans targeted by the AFL-CIO lost their re-election bids. At first glance, labor's effort looks like the disaster described by *The New Republic*. Labor failed to win back Congress, and given the widespread backlash against the congressional Republican agenda, even in districts where labor played no role (witness "B-1" Bob Dornan's defeat in Orange County, hardly a union bastion), it is difficult to make the case that the AFL-CIO was a pivotal actor in this year's elections.

But evaluated in other ways, the AFL-CIO's campaign effort brought a remarkable payoff. For one thing, it instantly snowballed into a massive free advertising campaign that unions would never have been able to afford without the cooperation of the media and their Republican foes. Dick Armey is hardly a popular figure these days, and when he says he wants to humiliate labor, it sets off warning bells for a lot of people who ordinarily don't give much thought to the subject. What was missed in the media's post-election coverage is that labor could not buy the 1996 elections, and labor leaders knew it. All that mattered was that Republicans needed a scapegoat, and the media have enthusiastically joined in labor's demonization.

Though it might not sound like it, this is a positive development. The more Republicans fulminate about "union bosses" and "big labor," the more they contribute to the perception that labor has a role to play in politics. And if labor is perceived as a major player, its issues become major issues. Union members strayed from the Democratic fold in the 1980s and early 1990s because Republican candidates were successful in bringing what are called "social issues" to the fore; union members were voting Republican because of things like gun control and abortion. But if union members can be reminded of the connection between their pocketbooks and their voting habits, they will come back together as a voting bloc. This is what the AFL-CIO aimed for, and what, to some degree, began to happen — with

the help of the Republican demonizers.

If Republican strategists want The Baffler's two cents, they would be better off simply ignoring the AFL-CIO. Fortunately for union sympathizers, our opinions don't count for much inside the Beltway.

Labor traditionally and correctly refuses to regard itself as just another interest group, as kin, say, to the NRA, or NFIB. But its 1996 campaign effort had much in common with the efforts of average interest groups, and it should be evaluated accordingly. No interest group can, by itself, buy elections; it can, however, buy access and recognition. Interest groups need plenty of help in order to affect national policy. Thanks to its 1996 effort, labor looks like it is in good position to get that help. In other words, measured by the criteria usually applied to interest group lobbying, labor's $35 million turns out to have been remarkably well-spent. Here's a simple crash course in interest group behavior to show why:

1. *Interest groups rarely make contributions solely to change the composition of Congress.* When they do try, they seldom succeed. Labor PACs are unusual in that they are among the largest and most partisan of PACs; historically, they have also given greater support to non-incumbent candidates than have other PACs. Yet they are still playing the same game other PACs play. A little known fact of the 1996 elections is that $3.2 million of labor's contributions went to (gasp!) Republicans; five of these Republicans defended their seats against Democrats who were *also* recipients of union contributions. Jack Quinn, who was re-elected to a Buffalo, New York seat, topped the list, parlaying his moderate voting record, his opposition to NAFTA and GATT, and his support for the Family and Medical Leave Act into $91,000 in labor contributions. New

Jersey's Bill Martini, labor's number two Republican with $69,000, did not fare so well; he lost by 3,000 votes to a labor-supported Democrat, William Pascrell. In both cases unions had their butts covered. Unions still need friends in the Republican Party, and they still have a few. Nor did the Republican power brokers have many personal battles with labor — virtually all of the 64 targeted Republicans were freshman or sophomore representatives. People like John Kasich, Henry Hyde, and even more powerful Republicans facing strong opponents, like Gingrich, didn't have to fight the AFL-CIO directly in their campaigns. When *The New Republic* cites Republicans who are plotting revenge, it pays scant attention to the fact that these are all relatively junior, powerless Republicans.

Political science-speak for what labor did is "buying access." It doesn't mean you get what you want from everyone; instead, it means you can walk in the door of your congressman's office without getting kicked out. It means that although the really tough kids, the committee chairs and the power brokers, might not do what you want, they won't be mad enough to pick fights with you. It also means that if you show the weak kids you can kick their ass, maybe next time they'll do what you want without putting up a fight. It means people will at least listen to you and try not to provoke you.

2. *For an interest group to maintain its own membership, it must be able to report to its members that their contributions made a difference.* A primary task for the AFL-CIO in this election was to persuade its members that their economic interests as workers and as union members were more important than other political concerns they might have. It had to persuade union members to think of themselves as union members first, and as Catholics or gun owners a distant second. The media and the Republican Party have been quite helpful here. The more credit unions get for their role in the election, the more the average union member will take pride in membership and equate the interests of the union with his or her own economic well-being. Take a close look at where union money went in this election: While the AFL-CIO did some independent expenditure on TV, most of what they did was phone-banking the membership on issues and trying to heal their divisions over single "social" issues.

"What they really zeroed in on was explaining to their own members policies as they related to job security and union positions at the bargaining table," says Wisconsin Democrat Lydia Spottswood, who was narrowly defeated by Mark Neumann in Wisconsin's First District. "They didn't want any of their membership going into the voting booth not knowing what it means when their representative votes for 'right to work' or 'team' legislation or to permit the permanent replacement of striking workers."

But if you're not a union member, you don't see this sort of behind-the-scenes work. So it's easy for commentators, junior media critics all, to misunderstand the AFL-CIO effort as a blunt attempt to buy the election.

3. *Current campaign finance laws virtually preclude the ability of any one group to have an effect on the outcome of elections.* Especially if that group only spends $35 million. Labor got attention because it told people how much it spent — and attention was exactly what it wanted to get. It's nearly impossible to tell how much other groups lavished on pet politicos; as the current Clinton brouhaha illustrates, soft money is hard to document. *Congressional Quarterly* estimates that business PACs outspent labor by a 7-to-1 margin; 70 percent of that money went to Republicans. And if

you scan FEC reports, you'll note that this doesn't include groups such as the mysteriously titled "Freedom Club," which bankrolled several Minnesota Republicans, and the even more nebulous "Committee to Reform," which poured money into the campaigns of several Illinois Republicans.

The AFL-CIO appears to have spent up to $500,000 in independent expenditures on TV commercials in some districts — naturally, Republicans drastically overstated how much was spent — yet even this was not necessarily enough to sway an election. Competitive races for Congress generally require a minimum of $700,000 in direct spending by each candidate; independent expenditures can often double this amount. Many Democratic challengers reported their frustration that whenever a soft money ad was aired in their district, Republicans were able to go out and raise more money to counter this ad almost instantly. Many of the targeted Republicans, including Cremeans, were able to go running to business groups and get soft-money ads to counter the AFL-CIO claims.

4. *Interest groups seldom have a real impact on elections, but it is to their advantage to claim that they do.* The most noticeable feature of the AFL-CIO's spending was that it put most of its money behind likely winners. The only link that can be drawn between all of the targeted Republicans is that they were all vulnerable. Some, such as Martini, were relatively friendly to labor. Others, such as Wisconsin Congressman Mark Neumann, were among labor's main enemies. But who received the most support from labor? Chicago's Rod Blagojevich, a virtual shoo-in against one-termer Michael Flanagan on the solidly Democratic North Side, former home of Dan Rostenkowski. Blagojevich would have won regardless of what labor did in his campaign. Meanwhile, the

AFL-CIO didn't bother to help several ardently pro-labor candidates in districts near Blagojevich's — and they all lost. This is a strategy that has drawn much criticism. One losing candidate told The Baffler:

Labor organizations only give money to the races they deem winnable. This is a position I take issue with, because if they don't mount efforts in races where their opponent has a history of being anti-union, how can they hope to raise the consciousness of people and to defeat anti-union thinking? The AFL-CIO needs to think more long-term about how to spend their money, because they can have more of an impact by even giving token contributions. You'd be surprised what a campaign like ours can do with $50.

"The AF of L being so outspoken about wanting to return organized labor but not doing anything to help me, when I'm running against their number one enemy, to me that's unprincipled," said another defeated Democrat. "When winning becomes more important than principle, then you've gone too far."

But politically, the decision not to help these candidates made sense. Most interest groups behave like this; you get credit for winning elections. Few would have cared if labor had helped several long-shot challengers get 45 percent of the vote instead of 25 percent. Challengers usually get only a little over 10 percent of the PAC money doled out in congressional races; while labor consistently gives more money to challengers than do other groups, it gave its money to people whose bandwagon it could ride, regardless of whether they needed the help or not.

5. *Campaign contributions seldom harm a group's goals.* Sitting on the

sidelines can, though. This is not political science, it is common sense, yet this principle is consistently disregarded by the media. Pundits from *The New Republic* to the *Washington Times* (certainly not as great an ideological leap as it once was) have grasped some of the above points, but they have looked in the wrong places to divine the effects of labor's campaign. Killian cites right-wing Wisconsinite Mark Neumann as an example of a Republican who, with the help of $1.4 million, beat the AFL-CIO-sponsored Spottswood and now vows vengeance. But consider these facts: Neumann eked out a narrow 2 percent victory in a district where one of three households contains a union member. He may talk tough in the company of other Republicans, but it would be political idiocy for him to spit on the interests of the 49 percent of voters who did not support his re-election. It would be a dare to unions to try harder next time.

Successful politicians moderate their positions, or at least their rhetoric, to reflect their districts. Neumann and many other Republican freshmen proudly refused to do so, but if the price of remaining far to the right of one's constituents is over a million dollars per election, some may change their minds. And contrary to *The New Republic*'s report, Neumann has in fact made a public show of just such an "aw, shucks, let's forget about the past and just be friends" demeanor since his victory. He broke ranks with his party early in the 105th Congress to vote against Newt Gingrich's re-election as speaker. And consider which Republicans have been most vocal about labor since election day. Cleveland's Martin Hoke has vociferously claimed that labor did him in; he can afford to, since he's looking for a job right now. Frank Cremeans has decried the distortions of his record perpetrated by the nefarious liberal elites; he's back in the concrete business now. Many of the Republican members of Congress whom Killian quotes are from districts with little union membership; Arizona's John Shadegg, for example, represents one of the most affluent and conservative districts in the state; he has little to lose from anti-union rhetoric.

This isn't to say that some Republicans don't want to get back at labor. The fact is that they won't, and probably can't. They can't beat labor in the direct manner favored by right-wingers in the past — by branding union activists radicals, by bemoaning the anti-democratic influence of union dollars while simultaneously raking in bucks from chambers of commerce everywhere. The Republican anti-labor stance of the 1980s succeeded by driving a wedge between union leaders and the rank and file, whipping up workers' anger at "elite" officials who spent their dues to further their own ambitions. The relative torpor of the Kirkland years let the Republicans get away with this, but the crucial thing to understand about the 1996 election is that this pseudo-populist brand of conservatism is showing signs of wearing thin. At the very least, the Republicans are showing signs of giving up on it. Either it doesn't work anymore or the congressional Republicans have forgotten how they got there. You choose.

Shortly after the election, the Cleveland *Plain Dealer* cited an AFL-CIO poll that showed that 72 percent of union members approved of the federation's political spending. This number raises the question of what was going on in the minds of those members — a minimum, by my calculations, of 7 percent — who voted Republican yet approved of labor's campaign. But if the AFL-CIO figures are in the ballpark (and they probably are), it looks like the Republicans are losing their ability to persuade union workers that their leaders are out of touch with them.

Appeals to workers on "social issues" might still be one way for the GOP to win their votes, but at the risk of alienating more affluent libertarian voters, the ones who do things like contribute to Republican candidates and join business PACs. The stalemated Republican agenda on "family" issues in the 104th Congress testifies to this quandary. The only other alternative is to try to change the laws so they specifically limit union spending. While the current campaign finance system is surely ripe for overhaul, the Republicans don't have the power to change it without limiting the power of their own PACs as well. Unions are already required to let their members know what percentage of their dues goes to political advocacy campaigns, and to give a partial refund if members ask for one. Republicans can try harder to publicize the refund option, but if the 72 percent figure is right, it wouldn't be worth the effort.

It is to labor's advantage to have congressional Republicans foaming at the mouth. Interest groups thrive on danger. Throughout the 1980s, liberals capitalized upon the threat Reagan and Bush posed to their interests; during the 1990s, countless right-wing groups have done the same thing with Clinton. As things have worked out this time, Republicans are a little scared and are responding the way unions want them to — talking about smashing labor while simultaneously trying hard to appease it behind the scenes. One of labor's pet projects for the next Congress, for example, is the passage of a health care package that would cover all American children currently without insurance. Look at the bill, and you'll be surprised to notice that Utah Sen. Orrin Hatch, who got a zero rating from the AFL-CIO in 1993 and 1994, is a sponsor. Meanwhile, as Republicans continue to talk about revenging themselves upon labor, and as the media continues to report on the trouble labor has gotten itself into, union members will become more, not less, supportive of labor's efforts to counter the GOP. John Sweeney won't tell you this, but it's true.

Republican rhetoric both misses the point and strengthens the AFL-CIO's position. If labor makes Republicans worried, it must have spent its money wisely. The Republicans would like to dismiss labor's role in the election, to have us believe that all the AFL-CIO netted was the scalps of 19 Republicans who might well have lost anyway. But then, they won't let it drop. Thirty-five million dollars, by itself, could never purchase as much free media time as labor has gotten. The AFL-CIO will tell you that its campaign was a success — and likely would have no matter what the outcome — but it was neither a success nor a failure, for any of the reasons offered by both sides in Congress and in the media. It wasn't necessarily even smart politics when you look strictly at the 1996 election results. It was, and continues to be, successful as an advertising blitz, an effort to bolster name recognition and product loyalty. If nothing else, labor demonstrated in 1996 that it has a dependable enemy.

Crazy Times Call for Repressive Organizations

Excerpts from Laborwatch, a monthly newsletter published by the Barens-Tate Consulting Group in Omaha, Nebraska:

Read the Signs: Unusual Activity Portends Union Organizing

Union organizing efforts come in all shapes, sizes — and degrees of stealth. Because unions vary strategies with employers, there is no one way to recognize when organizing is under way under your nose.

[...]

How can you tell if you're a target? many common behavioral patterns suggest organizational efforts. If you find any of these clues, you should strongly suspect union activity. Watch for:

• Unfriendly employees suddenly becoming unusually friendly to supervisors and managers.

• A sudden lack of communication between supervisors and normally friendly or conversant employees.

• New leaders emerging; different employees gaining recognition, attention and increased status and support from coworkers.

• Employees asking unusual questions about the company's structure, practices and policies.

• Unusual activity among groups of employees either before or after normal working hours.

• Employees continually congregating in small groups during working hours.

• Small groups of employees going to the washroom together.

• Unusual excitement during break times among employees.

• Increased contact among employees at their homes, whether or not involving outsiders.

• Professions of exceptional loyalty by recently hired employees.

[...]

There is no excuse for a union's organizing tactics to continue for very long without management's knowledge. Do not allow important indications of union activity to go unnoticed or uninvestigated. Remember: If you expose organizational efforts, you can counter them!

Don't Worry — Get Happy Employees to Ward Off Unions

Where do you rate on the union-tolerance scale? If you say "zero," then you need to zero in on ways to prevent your company form being a organizing target.

It's no secret that one reason employees turn to unions is job dissatisfaction. When workers are unhappy with their jobs (and, as a result, management), unions become an attractive alternative. Although you can't exert much control over unions, you can influence many "happiness" factors that lead to job satisfaction.

[...]

Supervisors who are unable to maintain positive relationships with subordinates will not gain the respect necessary to keep employees happy, productive and union free. We know that being a supervisor is hardly an easy task. Supervisors are stuck in between managers who demand and employees who question.

Your organization must provide necessary training to ensure that supervisors are effective. Train supervisors to demonstrate that they care, and that they will pass along employee concerns and ideas to management. This not only shows employees that someone is listening, but also gives management an ear to the ground.

If employees have the basic needs fulfilled that will make them happy in their jobs, usually they don't care who does it — the company or a union. If you come in first with positive steps to fill workers' happiness quotients, you can guess where that leaves unions on their "must have" scale (low).

Confronting the Capitalist International

David Moberg

W HEN she was 17 years old, Ana Alvarado fled the civil war in El Salvador for Los Angeles. Before long she was working as a maid at the luxurious New Otani Hotel, part of a Japanese chain owned by the Kajima Corporation, a transnational conglomerate whose main interests are in the construction business. Alvarado stuck with the job for 16 years, rising to the level of floor supervisor. She was unhappy with the pay, but even more so with management's response to workers' grievances. "Any time we complained," she says, "they showed us a bunch of applications. 'If you don't like it, walk out. We have more people who will work for less' " — mostly people like her, displaced by economic and political crisis in Mexico and Central America.

In 1995, Alvarado and a group of co-workers approached the Hotel Employees and Restaurant Employees International Union, but as their organizing campaign developed, Alvarado and 19 others were fired, clearly for their union activity. The union fought back. It mobilized Japanese community support in Los Angeles to block the award of a contract to build a new Japanese-American Museum to Kajima. It fought other Kajima projects, such as a bid to build a new high school, and it joined human rights advocates to promote bans on government contracts to businesses that operate in Burma, where Kajima has major interests.

The union also called for a boycott of the New Otani Hotel. Since most of the hotel's clients were from Japan, it sent a delegation, including Ana Alvarado, to Tokyo last December to meet with Japanese unions, leaflet the Japanese

Travel Bureau, present their case to Japanese tour companies, and link up with Japanese critics of Kajima's brutal use of forced Chinese labor during World War II. The U.S. delegation received expressions of support, but made few concrete gains. Then in April, AFL-CIO President John Sweeney went to Japan to demand neutrality from New Otani managers in the organizing drive. This was an important symbolic breakthrough, the first time that the leader of the U.S. labor movement has taken a direct role in a global labor dispute.

Ana Alvarado may be exceptional, but her situation is not. In the new global economy, hundreds of millions of workers are being cut adrift from their moorings — peasants displaced from the country to overcrowded cities and migrant workers seeking work in wealthier lands. The collapse of communism, free trade, technological innovations, and tougher management styles — all elements of the global economy — have destabilized industries and displaced millions of workers. None of this is entirely new to capitalism, but for Americans accustomed to stability and generalized affluence, the sharp recent rise in such displacement comes as something of a shock.

In addition, even as world trade increases, the expansion of direct foreign investment rises even faster. The World Trade Organization estimates that annual sales of foreign subsidiaries of transnational corporations now exceed the volume of international trade. The result is that workers, even those who are not employed by multinational corporations, face an economy that is not only more global but more dominated than ever by capital. In response, unions

sucky.investment.com

Highlights from the prospectus for
Wired's (first, failed) IPO, filed May 30,
1996. Brought from the SEC's
website to Baffler readers courtesy
of Doug Henwood.

THE COMPANY

Wired Ventures, Inc. (the "Company") is a new
kind of global, diversified media company engaged in
creating compelling, branded content with attitude for
print, online, and television. Its current businesses
include publishing Wired magazine and programming
original content on the World Wide Web (the "Web")
primarily through its HotWired network of online
content sites (the "HotWired Network"). The
Company believes that it has developed Wired and
HotWired into strong brands that symbolize new
media and the digital age.

[. . .]

Wired magazine was launched in January 1993
to cover the Digital Revolution, a term popularized by
the Company to describe the profound changes
caused by the convergence of the computer, media,
and communications industries. With Wired magazine's
blend of leading-edge editorial and highly innovative
design, the Company has created a unique magazine
genre. Wired magazine is not a computer magazine; it
is about the people, companies, and ideas of the
Digital Revolution.

[. . .]

LIMITED OPERATING HISTORY AND
ANTICIPATION OF LOSSES

The Company commenced the publishing of
Wired magazine in January 1993 and launched the
HotWired Network in October 1994. Accordingly,
the Company has a limited operating history upon
which an evaluation of the Company and its prospects
can be based. The Company has incurred operating
losses since inception, including operating losses of
$1.0 million for 1993, $3.5 million for 1994, $7.9
million for 1995, and $3.8 million for the three months
ended March 31, 1996. Partially as a result of a one-
time charge of approximately $21.3 million resulting
from the write-off of in-process research and
development pursuant to the Reorganization
described in "The Company," the Company expects
to incur a substantial loss for the three months ending
June 30, 1996. Moreover, deferred compensation
expense of $9.1 million relating to stock options
granted prior to May 31, 1996 will be recognized over
the four-year vesting periods of the options.

[. . .]

COMPETITION

The Company faces significant competition from
a large number of companies, many of which have
significantly greater financial, creative, technical, and
marketing resources than the Company. These
companies may be better positioned to compete in
the evolving media and technology industries. In
addition, the Company faces broad competition for
advertising revenue from other media companies that
produce magazines, newspapers, online content,
radio, and television, as well as other promotional
vehicles such as direct mail, coupons and billboard
advertising.

[. . .]

themselves are becoming more transnational. Most worker
conflicts with managers are still national or local, and that
isn't likely to change soon. But there are growing numbers of
cases like that of Ana Alvarado's, in which unions are
employing new tactics and finding new allies on a global
battlefield.

Unfortunately unions are playing catch-up in a contest
where they were once — a century ago — far ahead of business
in developing an international consciousness. During the 19th
century, unions helped not only to launch the various socialist
internationals, but also to establish the organizations now
known as international trade secretariats. International
worker movements split over the Russian revolution, however,
and then during the Cold War, American unions subordinated
their international work to supporting U.S. foreign policy and
fighting communism — and to fighting many leftist but non-
communist unions that crossed their path. American unions'
hard-line devotion to Cold War politics, which ranged from
supporting right-wing coups in Brazil to meddling in European
union politics, definitely served to divide and weaken the
international labor movement. But the Cold War had its up
side for the labor movement: As long as American unions were
zealously anti-communist, they found easy corporate allies,
friends in the CIA, and ready funding from the federal
government. Once Communism had collapsed, though,
businesses suddenly lost interest in "workers' rights" and
government funding dried up.

Now unions everywhere must rebuild international ties
from a position of relative weakness. New steps toward
international solidarity are changing labor movements
everywhere, perhaps most in the United States. But the tasks
ahead are daunting. Not only must unions organize workers
and take collective action on an unprecedented scale, they
must also conceptualize the new problems that workers face.

For the past 25 years, growing trade deficits have been
the main global-economic concern of most American unions.
In the years after World War II, when the United States was
the paramount industrial power, jobs were plentiful, and
unions felt they were included in the circles of political power.
Most unions supported free trade, but as the trade balance
turned negative in the late 1960s, many begun to favor what
they called "fair trade." That meant opening closed markets,
particularly in Japan, or erecting barriers against imports
deemed "unfair" (by which was meant, ironically, products that
benefited from industrial policies in other nations that unions
could only wish for in the United States). But unlike the free
market ideologues or the various corporations that denounced
German industrial subsidies, unions were interested in
promoting good jobs at home. They wanted to strengthen the
international hand of corporate "national champions," like

General Motors, General Electric, or Boeing, which employed American workers. If those companies flourished, it seemed, so would American workers.

European unions, it then appeared, had succeeded with such a strategy, though their home markets were also better protected from cheap foreign imports. Until the Thatcher era, even the most conservative European governments participated in formal or informal tripartite regimes with labor and business. But in the United States, where there was never much meaningful political corporatism, the need to piece together a global anti-Communist coalition through open markets trumped economic nationalism until the late 1980s. Government policy encouraged overseas investment by U.S. corporations, and in turn the corporations increasingly detached themselves from the United States. By the late 1970s, when American unions had come around to the European corporatist model, it was nearly impossible to find corporate champions that were clearly national.

Even when labor scored some "fair trade" victories for its brand of nationalism, they were incomplete or even backfired. In the case of the auto industry, the United Auto Workers won "voluntary" quotas on Japanese cars starting in the 1970s, whereupon Japanese manufacturers shifted to producing more profitable, bigger and more upscale cars, cutting into what had been safe markets for the Big Three. The Japanese also built more plants in the United States, as the UAW had demanded, but it turned out that Japanese automakers were extremely anti-union and even brought their anti-union auto parts partners with them, both of which seriously weakened the UAW. Then Japanese success spurred the Big Three to shift more of their production overseas and to Mexico as well as to accelerate their subcontracting of union jobs to lower-wage, non-union plants. Without quotas, union autoworkers would undoubtedly have been worse off, but quotas alone proved inadequate tools to protect their interests.

Then came NAFTA and the renegotiation of the General Agreement on Tariffs and Trade that created the World Trade Organization in 1994. Both of these made it clear that despite the rhetoric of free trade, regional and global agreements were mainly intended to liberate capital from certain government regulations and to enact other regulations to protect capital's rights on a global basis. Workers who had found it hard to make business socially accountable in their own countries were now faced with a global regime where they had almost no influence. But while most industrial union leaders knew they didn't like NAFTA from the start, the movement against NAFTA really grew from the grass roots, with the AFL-CIO only joining in popular mobilization late in the game. After NAFTA, the labor movement

MISSION AND STRATEGY

The Company aims to create smart media for smart people around the world — high-quality information and entertainment products aimed at a well-educated, affluent, technologically savvy, and influential consumer group. Its mission is to build a new kind of global, diversified media company for the 21st century utilizing its ability to create compelling, branded content with attitude across multiple media, its technological and research capabilities, its strong connection to consumers and advertisers, and its commitment to journalistic and artistic excellence.

The Company's strategy to achieve its mission includes the following elements:

CREATE SMART MEDIA FOR SMART PEOPLE AROUND THE WORLD.

The Company believes that creating high-quality information and entertainment products aimed at a well-educated, affluent, technologically savvy, and influential consumer group is the key to sustaining the rapid growth of its audiences, attracting advertisers, and maintaining advertising rates generally higher than those of its competitors. In addition, the Company believes that by focusing on a demographic group that includes today's thought leaders and early adopters of new ideas and technologies, it will also attract a broader group of consumers who are influenced by this group's ideas and viewpoints.

LEVERAGE EXISTING BRANDS AND CREATE NEW BRANDS.

The Company believes it has developed Wired, HotWired, and their related brands into brands that symbolize new media and the digital age. The Company intends to strengthen its existing brands by continuing to publish compelling print and online content for growing audiences and extending its existing brands across media including books and television. In addition, the Company intends to apply its creative resources and its expertise to develop new brands with distinct creative visions for print, online, and television. The Company believes that this diversification will enable it to create products that appeal to wider audiences with demographic characteristics similar to those of its existing consumers. The Company also believes that its HotWired Network and other online media properties provide a platform from which to rapidly and cost-effectively launch and test new brands, which can then be extended across media.

[. . .]

CAPITALIZE ON CONSUMER PROFILING CAPABILITIES.

The Company believes that its ability to target and develop relationships with its consumers will enhance the success of its media properties. In addition to collecting and maintaining profiles of its magazine readers, the Company uses proprietary technologies to obtain, manage, and analyze large amounts of volunteered or observed data regarding its online users. This information is then used by the Company's sales team in soliciting specific advertiser categories. It is also used by the Company's online advertisers to target particular users with advertising messages and by the Company to generate personalized editorial material for its online users. The Company also frequently surveys a panel of more than 20,000 online members that have volunteered to answer in-depth queries. The Company believes these capabilities enable it to develop and refine its own content, enhance the user's experience, and develop and strengthen its relationships with advertisers, thereby supporting its premium advertising rates.

internationally is placed in the difficult position of asking what kinds of regulation — if any — can be imposed on investment, and by whom.

In recent years, American unions have shifted their efforts from economic nationalism to protecting international labor rights and promoting international solidarity. Even in the NAFTA fight, the labor movement officially was not opposed to a regional pact in principle: Integration with Mexico was happening regardless, and unions simply insisted on a treaty that would protect Mexican workers' rights and raise their standards of living. Even unions that were once strongly protectionist, such as those in the garment and textile industry, had begun by the late 1980s to emphasize helping unions in Central America and the Caribbean organize workers in the sweatshop mini-states known as Export Processing Zones, places where unions are zealously suppressed.

Unions in the United States had long been accustomed to working with — though more often interfering with — unions in other countries, especially those that were poor and underdeveloped. But since the early 1980s, American unions have also come to see unions in other countries as crucial help in their own campaigns against corporations.

This has been part of a broader shift in American labor's foreign policy outlook. During the campaign against NAFTA, for example, U.S. unions found themselves at odds with their longtime ally in Mexico, a corrupt and undemocratic arm of the ruling party. Back in the 1980s, the union-backed National Labor Committee broke with Lane Kirkland's AFL-CIO and criticized the Reagan administration's Central American policies. That committee evolved into a group that now exposes Central American sweatshops that produce clothing for big U.S. retailers, such as Wal-Mart's Kathie Lee Gifford.

In the wake of NAFTA, a few U.S. unions have begun helping independent unions in Mexico to organize, especially when plants have closed and work has been moved to Mexico. Teamsters have sought Mexican allies to block the NAFTA trucking accord. In preparation for its big campaign to organize strawberry pickers this year in California, the United Farm Workers first sent organizers to Mexico in the winter to build support among workers who might be heading north in the following months. At the same time, unions such as the United Electrical Workers, UNITE, and the Laborers have brought in organizers from Mexico, Guatemala and even Bangladesh to help out in drives among immigrants at shops in the United States and Canada (playing a crucial role in a big organizing victory in Milwaukee, for example).

International solidarity has also become a new, though infrequently used, weapon in battles with transnational corporations doing business in the United States. In 1984, the United Mine Workers were forced into a long strike against A.T. Massey Coal, a company that was half-owned by Shell. Shell, of course, was a major pillar of the apartheid regime in South Africa and imported South African coal into the United States, facts which the UMW was able to turn against the multinational giant. The South African black miners' union also approached the UMW about support in its own battle against Shell, which arose from an incident in which mineworkers at a Shell operation had been forced back to work at gunpoint. The UMW decided to launch a boycott of Shell and recruited supporters from labor, anti-apartheid and other movements in the United States and Europe. It also managed to get South African coal banned from the United States for five years.

International solidarity has become an increasingly important tactic in all manner of less visible conflicts as well. When the Ravenswood Aluminum Corporation locked out steelworkers in Pennsylvania in 1990, European unions and one of the international trade secretariats helped the AFL-CIO track down financial fugitive Marc Rich, the ultimate power behind the company, who had holed up in Switzerland. The unions — including fledgling unions in Romania and Czechoslovakia — proceeded to protest and raise legal objections to new Rich ventures in their countries, eventually leading to a victory back in Pennsylvania. In 1995 and 1996 the Steelworkers developed an international campaign against Bridgestone/Firestone, the Japanese tire giant, which had brought in permanent replacements when U.S. workers had gone on strike. Though favorable National Labor Relations Board rulings allowed the union to extricate itself from a bad situation, Steelworkers President George Becker believes that the global labor actions — including high-level union delegations to managers, boycotts, and a couple of short strikes in other countries — convinced Bridgestone to settle. Likewise, when Paperworkers were locked out of a Danville, Illinois, factory in 1995 by owners that were part of a large Indonesian family empire, they linked up with East Timor human rights activists and Australian unionists, eventually forcing the company to bargain a reasonable contract.

Some international labor groups have begun to plan strategically on a global level, devising strategies to deal with particular companies or industries across national boundaries. In Europe, unions have long had to coordinate their efforts in such a manner, for example, to negotiate new mechanisms for consultation with workers that the European Union mandated for all transnational employers as part of the Maastricht agreement. Earlier this year, European and American union leaders met to discuss how they might extend those European Union mechanisms to the rest of the global operations of corporations affected by the European mandate.

Extreme Spreadsheet, Dude!

Excerpts from the prospectus for an initial public stock offering for VANS, a shoe and apparel company that caters to alienated suburban youth.

As a result of [its] reputation, the Company has developed a strong brand image which the Company believes represents the individualistic and outdoor lifestyle of its target customer base. The VANS brand image coincides with what the Company believes is a fundamental shift in the attitudes and lifestyles of young people worldwide, characterized by the rapid growth and acceptance of the alternative, outdoor sports and the desire to lead an individualistic, contemporary lifestyle. The Company believes that underlying factors influencing young people include: (i) programs broadcast worldwide on networks such as MTV, ESPN, and ESPN2; (ii) the growing international distribution and popularity of magazines such as Rolling Stone, TransWorld SKATEboarding, Spin and Details; and (iii) the increased independence and purchasing power of young people worldwide, as evidenced by the estimated 25 million teenagers in the United States who in 1994 spent approximately $89 billion.

[. . .]

To capitalize on the strength of the VANS brand with young men and women worldwide, the Company has recently repositioned itself from a domestic manufacturer to a market-driven company. With a focus on understanding the attitudes, lifestyle and product desires of its target consumer base, and by marketing and designing its product line accordingly, the Company believes it is well-positioned to further the growth of the VANS brand in this attractive market.

[. . .]

The Company's success is largely dependent on its ability to anticipate the rapidly changing fashion tastes of its customers and to provide merchandise that appeals to their preferences in a timely manner. There can be no assurance that the Company will respond in a timely manner to changes in consumer preferences or that the Company will successfully introduce new models and styles of footwear. Achieving market acceptance for new products may also require substantial marketing and product developments efforts and the expenditure of significant funds to create consumer demand. . . . The failure to introduce new products that gain market acceptance would have a material adverse effect on the Company's business, financial condition and results of operations, and could adversely affect the image of the VANS brand name.

[. . .]

Prior to fiscal 1995, the Company manufactured all of its footwear at two domestic manufacturing facilities located in Southern California. As part of the Company's strategic redirection, in the first quarter of fiscal 1995 the Company began to source from South Korea its line of casual and performance footwear known as the International Collection. The success of the International Collection created a domestic manufacturing overcapacity problem for the Company which contributed to an overstock in domestic inventories. In the second quarter of fiscal 1995, the Company increased the inventory valuation allowance from $324,772 to approximately $600,000 in order to help mitigate the risks associated with increased inventory balances. In the third quarter of fiscal 1995, the Company took steps to adjust its U.S. production; however, customer demand for the International Collection continued to grow. In the fourth quarter of fiscal 1995, it first became apparent that the domestic manufacturing workforce reductions would not be sufficient to address the increase in orders for the International Collection and the decrease in demand for domestically-produced footwear, and the Company determined that a plant closure would be required. Therefore, on May 30, 1995 the Board of Directors voted to close its Orange, California manufacturing facility (the "Orange Facility") and in July 1995, the Company closed the Orange facility. Accordingly, the Company recognized restructuring costs of $30.0 million in the fourth quarter of fiscal 1995. Of that amount: (i) $20.0 million represented a write-off of the goodwill allocated to the manufacturing know-how associated with the Orange Facility (the "Orange Facility Goodwill"). . . .

[. . .]

The Company's target customer segment is believed to have very favorable demographics. American Demographics magazine estimates that in 1995 there were approximately 29 million teenagers in the United States alone. This number is expected to increase to approximately 35 million by 2010, representing one of the fastest growing population segments. In addition, these target customers have substantial and increasing purchasing power. In 1994, teenagers spent an estimated $89 billion, of which $57 billion was money they earned themselves. Underscoring the importance of brand image, teenage boys participating in an American Demographics study responded that brand name mattered more in purchasing sneakers than when buying jeans, soft drinks or fast food.

[. . .]

This summer, the Company will be the exclusive sponsor of the "VANS Warped Tour '96."

[. . .]

The Company's casual and casual skate line includes ... the Razor™, Fracture™, Wally™, Rail™, Old Skool™, Era™, Mel™, and the Authentic™. . . . The Company believes the identification of its shoes with top skaters helps to increase sales of its performance footwear. Some of the Company's performance skate shoes are the Fairlane™, Ratz™ and Pudge™, as well as the Lo Cab™, Half Cab™, Mike Carroll™ and Salman Agah™ signature shoes. . . . Some of the Company's women's shoes include the Lucy™, Ethel™, Jinx™, Nice™ and Coodle™.

[. . .]

The Company sources the International Collection and snowboard boots from ten contractors in South Korea. During the first thirty-nine weeks of fiscal 1996, approximately 64% of the Company's shoes and 100% of the Company's boots were manufactured offshore by third party manufacturers.

Labor unions are a long way from being able to bargain on a global basis or even to think of conducting an international strike. It is often tough to coordinate efforts or get workers to support each other in one country, like the United States, or across all of Europe. It is harder yet for a worker in Italy to risk her job for another in Indonesia (or vice versa). Despite common basic interests — protecting the right to organize or raising living standards — workers in different countries do not always have identical short-term interests (such as where a new plant should be built). Even when international coordination could help them immensely — as in the disastrous struggle of Caterpillar workers earlier this decade in the United States — unions are often slow to recognize the need for global action.

Unions are also pursuing two other strategies to control transnationals. One aims to strengthen enforcement of basic labor rights — the right to organize and freedom from forced labor, child labor and discrimination — by linking those rights to all global economic arrangements, from the World Trade Organization to the World Bank to regional trade deals. As business pushes for new international rules on investment in the coming years, labor will insist that recognition of its rights be attached. Of course, many would like to ask for more — like a formula for raising minimum wages in countries as they develop — but most union strategists figure that even winning recognition of core labor rights will be difficult. To win anything in the international arena, though, labor must go beyond lobbying to mobilizing members globally for common political goals.

Second, since the point of the global economy is to permit corporations to evade regulation of any kind, whether by unions or by governments, unions are demanding that the rules of the new economy directly hold corporations — not just national governments — accountable for their social policies. One way of doing this is to transform existing voluntary codes of corporate conduct — now mainly a defensive public relations ploy — into a political arena in which business can be held accountable and workers can be permitted to bargain collectively. Another is to point out the contradiction between the hip, socially aware image of big apparel and shoe transnationals, like Nike or Donna Karan, and the fact that their products are usually made by sweatshop subcontractors.

The closest approach yet to a global collective bargaining agreement came after an international campaign in 1996 against child labor in soccer ball manufacturing. This campaign used both strategies and secured an agreement between the needle trades international trade secretariat and FIFA, the world soccer federation. That code of conduct, if implemented, will not only prohibit child labor but also

One Big Union For Capitalism
But Labor Must Stay in Its Own Back-Yard.

establish independent monitors, whose presence would in turn help protect the rights of adult workers to organize unions.

As countries respond to the global economy in different ways, free-fall into a laissez-faire market inferno is not as inevitable as it sometimes seems. For example, social-democratic traditions in continental Europe have dragged post-Thatcherite Britain toward greater accountability for business, which is one reason why British labor unions became more supportive of the European Union.

But even if workers around the world begin to see what they have in common with each other, they all live in distinct local environments with different needs. They have a stake in both local and national welfare, and any global regulation has to recognize those differences among nations and localities, as well as the common interest in rising standards of living, ecologically sustainable growth, greater social equality, and meaningful democracy. The rise of labor internationalism will not rule out the value or legitimacy of nationalist or localist sentiments, nor will it eliminate the potential disruption of international solidarity these sentiments can cause, as the European labor and social-democratic movements discovered in World War I. But internationalism will continue to temper and change national strategies of labor movements.

From local unions seeking alliances across borders to the AFL-CIO, where Sweeney's new leadership is clearing out the Cold War cobwebs and giving global solidarity new emphasis, the U.S. labor movement is groping toward new ways to deal with a global economy. So far, the successes have been few, but far too little has even been tried. Labor has learned that to win national labor struggles, it has to contest corporate rule at all levels, from shop floor to boardroom, from picket line to ballot box, and from local community to the mass media. It is even more necessary to do so when confronting global capital. The ability to disrupt the economy or a business is still critical for workers' power, but it is not the only source of strength.

Whatever the strategy, the clout of organized labor, even on a global scale, relies in the long run on deeply rooted, democratic organization and education of workers about the possibilities of a world in which money is the servant and not the master of their working lives. Now labor is in the very early stages of creating a new working-class culture of international awareness and solidarity. That change of outlook is not only critical for other strategies to work but is itself a source of power, just as the now-vanishing tradition of respect for picket lines once gave workers strength. If labor unions and their allies hope to overcome the threats to workers' well-being in the new global economy, they will have to advance their own vision of a unified world.

The More Things Change....
Peter Rachleff

TEN years ago, advocates of a revitalized labor movement heard our concerns echoed in the subtitle of Tom Geoghegan's book, *Which Side Are You On?: How to Be For Labor When It's Flat on Its Back*. Unions that had been at the center of the labor movement were shrinking in size and power, their members' wages and benefits sliding backwards, their jobs in peril. The very names of these unions — the United Mine Workers, the United Steel Workers, the United Auto Workers, the United Packinghouse Workers, the International Brotherhood of Teamsters — sounded like a bad joke. Unity, brotherhood, and solidarity seemed to exist only in the pages of labor history books.

The labor movement was cracking under the pressure of a joint offensive launched by corporate America and the Reagan-Bush administration. Plants were being closed, strikers were being "permanently replaced," and national union leaders appeared at a greater distance than ever from the men and women they were supposed to represent. The new jobs of the "Reagan revolution" were typically part-time, temporary, low-paying — and non-union. Year by year, the island of organized labor shrank smaller and smaller, while conditions on the island deteriorated. And the search for a viable response ran into one dead-end after another, leaving little but acrimony in its wake.

Here and there, rank-and-file anger and energy bubbled and threatened to break through the facade of impotency constructed by national union leaders. In 1985 and '86, Hormel workers in Minnesota fought a dramatic struggle against concessions. Their outreach efforts attracted the support of more than 3,000 local unions across America and union activists in 19 countries. But national union leaders, with the support of AFL-CIO officialdom, undermined their campaign, undercut their strike, eventually placing the local in trusteeship. Other struggles fared little better.

A dark cloud settled around the men and women who cared about the labor movement. We became an audience for grim, cynical expositions like Geoghegan's *Which Side Are You On?*, Ben Hamper's *Rivethead*, and Bill Serrin's *Homestead*. Documentary films — Michael Moore's *Roger and Me* and Barbara Koppel's *American Dream* — won acclaim while depicting workers as hapless victims of the late 20th-century corporate agenda, served up for the slaughter like rabbits and hogs.

In the early 1990s, NAFTA and GATT seemed to provide the final ingredients to a recipe for the eradication of the labor movement. Study after study pointed to lengthening workweeks, shrinking pay packets, growing ranks of working men and women without health benefits, the looting of pension funds, a growing contingent workforce, and a widening gap between the rich and the poor. If there hadn't still been union beer to cry in, we labor advocates would have been in an utterly hopeless situation!

But just as we seemed ready to give in to despair, the mass media and the AFL-CIO's own public relations spinmasters have begun to inform us that the labor movement is back. For the sports fans among us, it has all the feel of a bottom-of-the-ninth rally, a Hail Mary pass into the end zone, a desperation three-pointer as the clock ticks off the final seconds.

Organized labor's chiliastic revival supposedly began with the election of John Sweeney, Richard Trumka, and Linda Chavez-Thompson to the leadership of the AFL-CIO in October 1995. The "New Voice" slate's millennium would be ushered in with well-conceived strategies, militant tactics, energetic organizing, and new coalitions. The shame of the Caterpillar capitulation would be washed away with a tidal wave of "Union Summer" organizers.

The prophets of a revitalized labor movement crowed loud and long this summer and fall. "Union Summer," they claimed, would bolster the new leadership's agenda to organize the unorganized. Bright, idealistic, energetic college students would help sign up thousands of new members. At the same time, the AFL-CIO would launch a $35 million campaign to defeat anti-labor congressmen and senators in the fall elections. The same prophets hailed the "new alliance" of intellectuals and labor leaders signaled by the October 1996 labor teach-in at Columbia University.

But recent events suggest that the words of the "New Voice" have a familiar, ashy taste. "Union Summer" may well have awakened an impressive coterie of college students to the potential power of a renewed labor movement, but there have been few tangible results to point to. Meanwhile, the corporatization of higher education itself continues, as public universities privatize hospitals, resist clerical workers' demands for decent wages and respectful treatment, and crush graduate employees' efforts to organize. The AFL-CIO's electoral strategy bore little fruit, save for the backlash it provoked. The very Republicans labor failed to unseat have introduced a bill that would severely restrict unions' right to spend members' dues dollars on political activity.

Events so far in 1997 suggest that the changes in the AFL-CIO leadership are amounting to the "same old, same old." The unions engaged in the prolonged Detroit newspapers strike have waved the white flag. Their offer of an "unconditional return to work" rings hollow, given that, with "permanent replacements" on the job, there is no

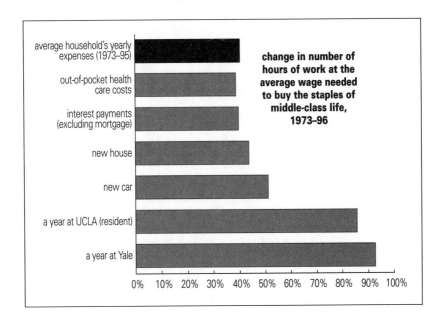

change in number of hours of work at the average wage needed to buy the staples of middle-class life, 1973–96

average household's yearly expenses (1973–95)
out-of-pocket health care costs
interest payments (excluding mortgage)
new house
new car
a year at UCLA (resident)
a year at Yale

0% 10% 20% 30% 40% 50% 60% 70% 80% 90% 100%

work to return to. The unions now pin their hopes on favorable judgments on a long list of pending "unfair labor practice" complaints filed with the National Labor Relations Board. Favorable rulings could mean sizeable back-pay settlements, to be sure. But ask any worker who has waited — or is still waiting — to receive justice through this slow, ineffective process. Just ask the Caterpillar strikers or the locked-out Staley workers about how assiduously the Labor Board protected their rights. They'll laugh.

The Detroit strikers themselves and their many supporters around the country suspect that the "leadership" opted to end the strike rather than respond to the growing groundswell for a national labor march in Detroit. For months last winter, unionists and other activists wrote or called AFL-CIO leaders to demand that they call such a march. The federation relented, slating a march on Detroit for June, but only after union leaders called off the strike altogether.

The same week, President Clinton invoked the Railway Labor Act to block the imminent American Airlines pilots' strike. I suppose it's no revelation that: (1) in the new, "deregulated" economy, only labor is still regulated; (2) workers only have the right to strike when its exercise can be expected to be ineffective; and (3) the AFL-CIO leadership may be a "Friend of Bill," putting material and human resources in the cause of his re-election, but Bill cannot be counted upon as a friend of labor. No revelation, perhaps, but surely disquieting for those who prophesy a new dawn for the labor movement. Rather than speaking of a cloud lifting, it might make more sense to speak of the smoke clearing. That is, at the top of the AFL-CIO, the more things have changed, the more they have stayed the same.

Fortunately, however, this is not the whole story for labor in 1997, any more than the defeats of the 1980s and early 1990s were all there was to the Lane Kirkland era. Beneath the surface, outside of the media spotlight, a new labor movement has been struggling to take shape, to define itself, to burst forth. The Hormel strike showed some of the contours of this new movement — defined by the rank and file, militant, eager to reach out not only to other local unions but to organizations outside the labor movement, willing to experiment with tactics beyond picket lines, such as product boycotts and pressure on employers' financial allies.

Other local unions adopted similar tactics in the late 1980s. Some were quite successful in energizing their own members, in building horizontal solidarity networks, and in forging local coalitions. Typically, however, they came up short. All too often, they engendered the enmity of their own international unions, who continued to resist locals' efforts to militantly confront employers.

In some unions, movements blossomed to challenge their national "leadership." The most impressive of these reform movements was Teamsters for a Democratic Union (TDU), which led the way in transforming their own union. When the government threatened to prosecute the Teamsters under the Racketeer Influenced and Corrupt Organizations Act, TDU was able to push for internal reforms such as the direct election of the union's national officers. They helped elect a reform-minded president, Ron Carey, and to push for additional procedural reforms and progressive measures that have made the Teamsters the labor movement's biggest success story.

When the threat of NAFTA emerged in the early 1990s, several local unions broke with traditional protectionism to promote a new international solidarity. Several of these locals, together with the small but feisty United Electrical Workers, participated in international conferences, engaged in solidarity actions with Mexican and Canadian fellow unions, and undercut the nationalism and racism that had once been widespread among their own rank-and-file members.

Promising developments also took shape within unions whose members — white-collar workers, public employees, women, workers of color, immigrants — had never been part of organized labor's mainstream and had never been completely integrated into the mainstream model of business unionism. These unions adopted techniques to promote rank-and-file participation, strategies to avoid reliance on grievance procedures and standard arbitration, and tactics that engaged the outside community directly. They found new energy in these efforts, and they became models for other labor activists who sought paths out of the darkness in which they had long been mired.

Even further out at the margins, new organizations are pushing at the very forms of unions, creating "workers' centers," "non-majority status unions," and "unofficial central labor bodies." Organizations such as Black Workers for Justice in North Carolina, the Chinese Staff and Workers Association in New York City, Asian Immigrant Women Advocates in Oakland, the Immigrant Workers Resource Center in Boston, Korean Immigrant Workers Advocates in Los Angeles, La Mujer Obrera in El Paso, and the Southwest Florida Farmworkers Project reflect the self-organization of workers long ignored by the main-stream labor movement. They involve their communities in workplace struggles and bring workers as a collective force into community struggles.

Conferences of various sorts have brought many of these activists together

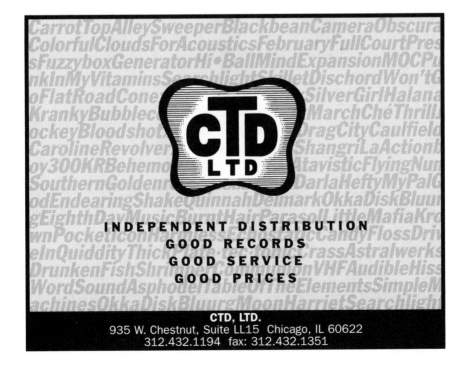

to share experiences and learn from each other. In Detroit, *Labor Notes* magazine hosts a biannual conference that attracts more than 1,000 self-identified "troublemakers." In panels and workshops, these men and women disseminate practical strategies, explore new ideas, and promote networking within industries and regions.

In the Twin Cities, the annual "Meeting the Challenge" conference has provided hundreds of Minnesota unionists with access to veterans of labor's new wave — men and women, in the words of one conference organizer, who "do not live and work separately from the workers they are talking about." In February 1997, as the AFL-CIO leadership was again stumbling, conference participants met others involved in the following: the Hotel and Restaurant Workers in Las Vegas, who have doubled the size of their local to 40,000 members in the past decade; the California Nurses Association, which has used the petition and referendum process to save nurses' jobs and put forward health care reform that looks out for patients' interests; an organization of 5,000 newly organized African-American women in the Mississippi catfish processing industry; and the clerical workers union at Harvard University, which has energized its membership with creative, even fun, tactics that remind the administration that workers make the elite university run on a daily basis.

As yet, these diverse grassroots movements have neither shifted the direction of the mainstream labor movement nor coalesced into a new movement of their own. But their vitality suggests that the labor movement is far from "flat on its back." They may be outside the spotlight of the mass media, opaque to the academic cheerleaders for the AFL-CIO's new leadership, but they hold our future in their hands. We need to learn more about these movements, help connect them with each other, and tell their stories every chance we get.

Three Scenes From a Bull Market

Josh Mason

"I'm a Marxist. But more importantly, I'm an entrepreneur."

— *Sander Hicks, quoted in* Green

I. Extraordinary Popular Delusions

EVERY Friday evening, a rumpled thirtyish young man in a badly-fitting suit jacket dispenses stock picks on CNNfn. He's a columnist for *Worth* magazine, and publisher of a successful financial-advice newsletter. No surprises there — except to veterans of the Chicago rock scene, who may rub their eyes when they see "Ken Kurson" flashing at the bottom of the screen. Hey, didn't he used to be front man for the Lilacs? Sure was — and before that, bassist for Green, a musically uninteresting but moderately successful Eighties pop band, from which he's taken the name for his newsletter. At first glance it looks like the Repo Man scenario: punk rocker, with serious misgivings, gone to work for The Man. And it is, minus the misgivings — and with some strange complications.

Green, according to the manifesto that Ken Kurson includes in every issue, is a financial newsletter "for the rest of us — those who know that 'the man' really couldn't care less if we young 'uns approve of his larceny. . . . for those who don't care how cool it is to admit that they care about their lives and their futures." As it turns out, *Green's* operational definition of caring about your life and future is: *Buy mutual funds. Green* operates under the odd conceit that shilling for mutual funds is, as the passage just quoted suggests, a daring and transgressive act — or, in Kurson's words, "*Green* is based on the premise that moneytalk is the last

taboo." Thus, we learn that by explaining what bonds are *Green* is "tilting at windmills." And in an interview with pornographer Al Goldstein, *Green* informs him that "Pornography doesn't shock as much as it used to, but trying to get people to talk about how much they make, what they invest in, how much they've lost is as cumbersome as 'Who have you slept with?' once was."

Of course, The Man does care if we approve of his larceny; for proof, look no further than Kurson, whose vocal and enthusiastic approval has been rewarded with a cushy columnist's gig at *Worth* and a regular spot on CNNfn, as well as a book contract fat enough to buy him a house in New Jersey. From its beginnings in 1995 as "The Kenny Quarterly," a xeroxed, stapled newsletter sent out to Kurson's friends and acquaintances, *Green* has grown into a glossy magazine with a circulation of some 15,000 and a prominent spot on the magazine racks of literary bookstores that wouldn't deign to stock run-of-the-mill financial magazines. The magazine's web site and promotional materials are decorated with literally dozens of fawning blurbs from places like the *Chicago Tribune* and the *Orange County Register* as well as *Raygun* and *Spin*.

What's the secret? It's sure not the advice. An ad for the magazine suggests that you'll find *Green* useful "if you don't know exactly what a mutual fund is." This is correct. If you are familiar with the concept of mutual funds, though, it's

Ursus Wallstreetus

Doug Henwood

Last January, I got a call from Jim Grant, editor of **Grant's Interest Rate Observer**, a Wall Street newsletter on the credit markets. Jim was a bit nervous that the dockers strike in Liverpool had attracted sympathy strikes, demonstrations, and other actions around the world — a solidarity campaign organized in part through the Internet. The rise of labor is always bad for the bond market, and Jim was afraid that in all the hype about fiber optics, it'd been forgotten that rebellious proles can get wired too. Was the historical tide of the last 20 years reversing itself, and labor beginning to rise again?

It was my duty to tell Jim that labor's attempts at international solidarity, as inspiring as they are, have typically burned out quickly. Maybe someday a global labor movement could sustain itself, and if it did, it'd certainly be wired, but it'd also use phones and letters too.

Ursus Wallstreetus is a strange species. Almost without exception, bears adore capitalism as the most wonderful institution that humans have ever devised, the goal of all social evolution. But the true bear — not the temporary cyclical bear, but the temperamental permabear — always expects all kinds of disasters: inflation, deflation, boom, collapse, in turn or in various strange combinations. Whatever seems a plausible reason for a sharp and sustained drop in security prices will do. Aside from a few catastrophist Trotskyist sects, Wall Street bears are virtually the only people in America who have faith in an imminent labor uprising.

Though stockbrokers can often be

far from clear what you'll learn from reading *Green*. Typical nuggets include answers to questions like "What's a bond?" (this topic seems to be covered in every issue, but it merits feature-length treatment in #3) or "What's a stock split?" (it's when a stock splits). My personal favorite: "Unlike growth funds, which seek companies based on their growth prospects, 'value' funds troll [sic] for companies whose stock is, in the opinion of the fund manager, undervalued." Got it? It takes three pages in #2 to demonstrate that if you owe money on several credit cards, you should pay off the one with the highest interest rate first.

What sets *Green* apart are its treatises on the hipness and even the morality of investing: Mutual funds are what separates the men from the boys, the sole alternative to a lifetime of humiliating dependence on one's parents. Kurson's manifesto is worth quoting at length:

> *Green* was conceived because its editor is frequently asked about finance by friends, coworkers and relatives, a diverse gaggle who share only one thing in common: None would ever be caught dead trying to master something as uncool as money. It's not punk rock, it's not rebellious, it's something of which my parents might approve, whatever. So they wallow in financial purgatory, ringing up astronomical debts on credit cards and student loans, many of which are taken to finance education in vanity disciplines that will never pay enough to make good on the loans. That's not rebellion and it's not freedom. It is the modus operandi of privileged and spoiled kids who know their parents will bail them out when things get too rough.

Well, *is* money punk rock? The question is answered by an interview with Circle Jerks drummer Keith Clark, who moonlights as a tax accountant. Getting the relation between youth culture and stock ownership right has been a vexing problem for the authors of the vast literature on Gen X, torn as they are between the fantasy that twentysomethings are a uniquely frugal generation who will save the stock market and the fear that they've been spoiled by Social Security and commercial TV. Kurson himself is sharply divided on this subject: On the one hand, it's the frugal Gen Xers who are supposed to be his readers, but on the other, he regularly berates his peers as pampered and indolent. (This contradiction is nicely captured in the manifesto, where *Green* is first "conceived" for Kurson's "friends, coworkers and relatives," but by the end is "not for them" since they are, every one of them, whiny mama's boys and girls.) In his TV and radio appearances, where he is invariably treated by interviewers as envoy and interpreter for the mysterious tribe of Youth, Kurson prefers to talk about how much his generation loves to save: "I think people in Generation X, to use an overused term, feel that the Social Security system is by no means guaranteed to be around by the time they retire, that self-directed retirement plans, 401(k)s and IRAs, are really mandatory now." But in the privacy of his own pages, he's more liable to vent his rage against the popular kids who mocked him for his forbidden love of Mammon. "I had to be very secretive about my interest in money," he recalls, looking back at those painful years. "I've been at parties where people are discussing every kind of perversion and admiring the host's Gacy paintings, but just try to bring up compound interest and watch the room clear."

The kids are wise; the kids are fools. The nadir comes in *Green* #4, the women's issue (the cover of which bears the thoughtful slogan, "This One's for the Ladies"). First, there's an interview with two strippers, who, it turns out, are entrepreneurs who "know more about sales, marketing and finance than the businessmen they entertain for a living." Then there's Kurson's bizarre take on star *New Republic* plagiarist Ruth Shalit: In a spasm of generational rancor (and without any evidence, textual or otherwise), he blames Shalit's thievery on . . . *those damn slackers*. "I think she steals because she's angry. I believe that Ms. Shalit hates that she has no time to relax. That she has to use her good looks and charm to get what should be hers because of her talent alone. . . . Her transgressions owe their origin to a bitterness at the cynicism and laziness of too many people her age." The essay simultaneously hits new lows both in its celebration of personal irresponsibility and its disdain for the non-greedy. "Ambition is a dirty word these days," Kurson ludicrously observes of the world that gave us Shalit, incensed that anyone — anyone — out there could put their muse or peace of mind before filthy lucre.

What is it about *Green*'s self-contradicting mass of resentment and bragadoccio, its thoroughly scrambled ideas of social class (Kurson, the *soi-disant* working-class kid, dispenses instructions on how to deal with "jagoff waiters" and boasts about acquaintances who, ever so classily, "serve sandwiches on linen napkins"), that has so caught the ear of Wall Street's image masters?

And when else but during the most superstitious of bull markets could a writer with a total lack of qualifications to offer investment advice make up for it with nothing but stylish (Kurson has style in spades) expressions of ingenuous, almost infantile, wonder at the institutions and public mores of capitalism? Kurson is continually agog at the fact that under capitalism you don't necessarily have to work for money, you can compel money to work for you. Each of the first few issues of *Green* featured a little panegyric on interest,

giddily optimistic, a sizeable portion of Wall Street, especially those around the bond market, are staunch partisans of gloom, if not outright doom. Gloom is as much a part of the bondbroker's sales effort as optimism is of the stockbroker's. Bond investors love sluggish economies and servile workers; anything that threatens these two factors, like strong growth and tight labor markets, is regarded with alarm. So it's not surprising that the overall culture of rentiers and traders is often gloomy, even sadistic. Daily newspapers have so absorbed this worldview that drops in unemployment are described as "alarming" (the **New York Times**), and a low rate of unemployment something against which experts "warn" (**Washington Post**).

Since stocks rarely do well if the bond market isn't, mainstream Wall Street wants a happy bond market. So if selling securities is your business, then you don't want to have economists department forecasting strong economic growth. This made for trouble in 1993-1997, when the U.S. economy often showed far stronger growth than Wall Street predicted or wanted. One economist who was rightly forecasting growth above the Wall Street consensus in 1993 and 1994 was called in by his boss and told to mark down his numbers. Meanwhile, Ed Hyman, Wall Street's favorite economist (according to the **Institutional Investor** poll, which he won for about a dozen straight years), predicted all sorts of slowdowns that never materialized. By coincidence, in addition to sending out his own commentaries and forecasts, Hyman also sells bonds and manages a large bond portfolio.

Most of the time, these hacks are rarely called to account for their bad forecasts. A rare and delicious moment, however, came in late 1994. Every January, the **Wall Street Journal** does a roundup of predictions for the coming year. One of the most prominent gloomsters on the Street, Phil Braverman, had predicted that 1994 would be a year of a torpid economy, meaning lower interest rates and an indulgent Federal Reserve. Instead, the economy proved strong (strong, that is, by the standards of the last 20 years, not those of Golden Age America or East Asia today) and the Fed tightened six times during the year. Asked to explain what went wrong, Braverman replied that he hadn't made the mistake, the Fed did.

The most intriguing form of bear is the one gunning for a generalized financial collapse. Many, if not most, permabears hew to some brand of right-wing political economy, and blame the always-imminent disaster on various statist perversions of The Free Market. (Their notion of a pure stateless ur-market is, of course, complete fantasy; it's always taken powerful states to create markets and keep them from spinning out of control.) Some are "Austrians" — followers of Hayek and von Mises, who hold, among other things, that the ceaseless extension of credit, supported by indulgent central banks, leads to vertiginous booms and punishing busts. Central banks are, of course, institutions of the hated state, which prevents the body economic from undergoing a ritual depressive purge every 10 or 20 years. Sure, such a purge would bankrupt millions and drive the unemployment rate up toward 20 percent, but that's just one of the unpleasantries of life. If you don't let the purifying ritual of depression do its purgative work now and then, the consequences will be even worse — the inevitable crash that never seems to arrive.

Probably the most entertaining bears are the lunatics who inhabit the edges of respectability. One of the looniest such outposts is the newsletter Strategic Investment, edited by James

with titles like — no kidding — "The magic and beauty of compound interest" and "The glory and magic of compound interest, redux." Of course there's plenty of talk about self-reliance, but it turns out that self-reliance is something you do with your stocks. Indeed, to read this stuff you'd think the world contained no one but bed-ridden invalids pampered round the clock by private nurses, and brawny loners forging their way through the world with nought but two strong arms and a well-balanced portfolio.

Most importantly, investing in stocks is said to be the only assurance of happiness when your own earning power falters, especially in retirement, which is, after all, what the money is being saved for. (Kurson doesn't believe in Social Security, but more on that later.) Obviously, Kurson is not the first to notice that, as he puts it, "Freedom means money." What's new is his discovery that, with the right packaging, independence, self-reliance, and autonomy — in short, adulthood — can be purchased from a brokerage. It's almost clever enough to justify all the money he's made.

But all that stuff about stocks and compound interest is for people who don't know the game of ideology as well as Ken Kurson. The real way to make money in a bull market isn't mutual funds, it's working up a highly visible enthusiasm for mutual funds, letting yourself be seen reinventing the wheel of capitalist ideology in the language and garb of Generation X.

The most important element of that ideology, of course, is the political. Criticizing an article in *Harper's* expressing skepticism at the idea that stock investing can replace our current system of public provision for retirement, *Green* says, "It's difficult to see why he's wringing his hands. Sure, it'd be wonderful if some benevolent government or corporation were genuinely looking out for us," but it just ain't so. "Better to know the score while there's still time to stuff your mattress." That's our choice, kids: benevolence from on high, or mattress-stuffing down below. If we can't count on our leaders to care for us, then it's every man for himself and devil take the hindmost. Notice what's excluded here: the possibility of any kind of collective, political action. But that — not government "benevolence" — is where Social Security and employer-provided pensions and the rest of it came from in the first place, and that's the only kind of action most people can take to ensure their well-being 40 years down the road.

II. Tulipomania

W̲ITH an unbending moral code balanced by a promise of plenty in the hereafter, the speculation craze, whipped into a frenzy by the many investment-advice publications that have sprouted during Wall Street's long sunny season, has all the makings of a vernacular American religion. True to form, the ebullient promoters like *Green* even have dark alter egos following in their wake, a platoon of Jeremiahs whose abiding fear is that even the gravity-defying market of the Nineties has not drawn in *enough* money. With the feverish intensity of street-corner preachers, they collar any passerby foolish enough to make eye contact, pressing the literature into their hands with an impassioned plea: Jesus saves, and so should you.

The high priest of this cult is undoubtedly Pete Peterson, multimillionaire investor and advisor to a half-dozen presidents, whose brief is for probity, parsimony, and self-abnegation. "People may think this will be painless," he likes to say. "It won't." His obsession, as he let the world know in his 1996 book, *Will America Grow Up Before It Grows Old*, is aging: He's convinced that "demographics is destiny." The argument — and admittedly, it's at least superficially compelling — goes like this: The country is getting older, people are living longer and having fewer children (an average of two per couple, compared with three or more during the Fifties). This "age wave" will mean many more unproductive retirees with expensive health care and nursing home habits, and fewer workers to pay for them. It also will mean a much bigger bill for government programs for the elderly, like Social Security and Medicare.

As it turns out, the "age wave" is a remarkably easy fear to debunk. While it's true that there are more old people than ever, the number of children and housewives (the rest of the dependent population) is decreasing; in fact, the ratio of non-workers to workers has dropped steadily over the past century and is now at its lowest point ever. Honest fiscal conservatives should take as their slogan "No more housewives!" But these facts don't interest Pete Peterson. For him, the demographic story is just a hook on which to hang his view of the world: a vast struggle between the forces of good and evil, where to be good is to save and to be evil, to spend. "When I was a child," he lectures the impecunious boys and girls of today, "I witnessed first-hand what can be accomplished by parents who dedicate themselves to posterity. For decades on end, my father, in Kearney, Nebraska, kept his small restaurant open 24 hours a day, 365 days a year. Every penny that didn't cover necessities or get plowed back into the business he set aside for his children's future. To him, being called a 'big spender' was the ultimate insult."

Like most of his ilk, Peterson emplots his narrative (as the historians say) into a tale of psychocultural decline. As with theirs, the self-indulgent Sixties play no small role in his story, but he goes back further: to the end of World War II, when an America besotted with its own strength abandoned the thrift (the word derives from "to thrive,"

Dale Davidson and Lord William Rees-Mogg. Davidson, who also runs a loopy anti-tax foundation, is constantly scouring the globe for a retreat in case of global meltdown; right now, his favorite potential retreat is one in the "delightful green hills" of New Zealand. Meanwhile, virtually every issue includes a dispatch from house stock market pundit Michael Belkin declaring the great bull market of the 1980s and 1990s to be already over. Every additional 1000 points tacked onto the Dow simply serves as further confirmation of the crash's imminence. In his more fevered moments, Belkin circulates tales of the Fed's "safe houses," from which Alan Greenspan's agents buy stock index futures to boost the market whenever it sags.

Wall Street is supposed to be a place of great sophistication. In one sense this reputation is deserved; it takes a certain degree of imagination and technical skill to devise instruments like inverse floaters, poison put bonds, and remarketed reset notes. But when it comes to political and economic analysis, denizens of the Street are as crude as any barroom philosopher. All of which might be overlooked if Wall Street's bears came up with better investing advice or pleaded allegiance to higher truths. Unfortunately, they live in a world that knows no higher truth than statements of profit and loss.

M.O.

Peterson helpfully reminds us) his father practiced in the Thirties and Forties. Did Peterson expect birthday presents when he was boy? Not a chance! Just "a small metal barrel with a slot in the top — a 'gift' from a local S & L — in which my brother and I were expected to save our pennies, nickels, and dimes. My parents assumed we would make regular trips to this local S & L and deposit these savings for our future." Peterson's obsessive mind draws him into some strange alliances. Unlike other conservatives, he's pro-public television, at least for children, because it offers an alternative to commercial TV's "endless commercials, all telling them to 'buy now.'" From his point of view, victory in World War II wasn't worth the moral cost for this country. Convinced they had won the war, Americans grew proud and lazy, insisting on working shorter hours for higher wages, which they furthermore insisted on spending rather than turning over to the trusty neighborhood S & L.

But now, Peterson insists, with the country soon to be overflowing with geezers, we're in for our comeuppance. No more entitlements, not for the poor, and not for the middle class either. No more assuming you deserve a decent job, a home, an education. And certainly no more assuming you deserve to retire. Peterson points admiringly at the Japanese, who, "unlike Americans, ... are un-encumbered by the idea that people are entitled to live the last third of their adult lives in subsidized leisure." Never mind that Peterson nearly doubles what is in fact the average length of retirement; the sight of anyone lazing around in retirement homes fills him with fury. Those people should be out flipping hamburgers!

But it's not just retirees who will have to bear the burden — we'll all have to tighten our belts and save like madmen. Only by saving and investing, Peterson assures us, will we be able to fill the insatiable maws of "a nation of Floridas." Some people may think "this will be painless," he cackles. "It won't.... There are no free lunches! To save more, we must consume less."

But does productive investment really depend on increased savings? The short answer is no (for the long answer, check out Doug Henwood's book *Wall Street*). According to John Maynard Keynes — and to the best evidence available today — investment is constrained not by a lack of savings but by a lack of sufficiently profitable investment opportunities. The typical big modern corporation is swimming in capital but demands a 10, 11, or 12 percent return before investing in plant or equipment on a significant scale. Such returns are understandably hard to come

When you are songwriting

David Berman

by. Saving more and consuming less will merely make them rarer still, and leave us poorer, not richer, when the Baby Boomers retire.

Bad economics though they may be, calls for increased saving have an undeniable emotional resonance for some. Certainly this is the cathexis *Green* is tapping into. For younger observers, though, there's something just a little odd about the idea of people in their twenties obsessing over retirement. I have no idea what I'll be doing in four years, let alone in 40; it's as likely as not that life as we know it will by then have been brought to a halt by global war or ecological collapse (or, if you believe the techno-futurists, have been transformed into one continuous virtual orgasm). It's a safe bet that what's really on the mind of *Green* readers is not the size of their bank account in 2040 but its size today, and for all the usual reasons, punk rock or not. But let's take the Peterson/*Green* program at face value: Is it true that how much you save and invest when you're young is the main determinant of your standard of living when you're old?

The answer is, No. Not to put too fine a point on it, they've got it exactly backwards. For the vast majority of people, private saving does not contribute significantly to income in retirement. From all the millions of words devoted each year to saving for retirement, you'd never guess what a small proportion of most people's retirement income such saving actually represents. Barely 10 percent of the income of the typical elderly household consists of income from assets — and an unknown but significant portion of this represents payments from defined-contribution pension plans rather than private saving per se. Nor does this calculation take account of Medicare and Medicaid (the latter pays for nursing homes). If they were included, the proportion of income the elderly receive from investments would be smaller still.

Looked at another way, if you measure the average income from the four major sources — earnings, Social Security, income from assets, and pensions — for elderly households with each type of income, income from assets ranks dead last, at about $1,700 per year.

In other words, your investments — the only ones that count — are a job with a decent employer who provides a pension, and belonging to a society civilized enough to take care of its members' essential needs. According to *Green*, though, all that is going to evaporate one of these days ("the Social Security system is by no means guaranteed to be around") but, hey, banks and bull markets are forever!

III. The Madness of Crowds

I read somewhere that the attribution of the line "Let them eat cake" to Marie Antoinette is unfair; the French word she used really referred to a cheaper kind of flour (a better translation might be, "Let them eat Wonder Bread"). Those who say, in the words of a recent *New Republic* headline, "Let them eat stock," have no such excuse: They mean exactly what they say. James Cramer, who wrote the *New Republic* piece, seriously suggested that the solution to layoffs is to give the fired workers stock options: "No government intervention is needed; it would be voluntary, but, once a handful of companies adopt these packages, all will follow." Talk about market magic: The bull market solves for alienated youth, for a nation of dead-weight oldsters, and now, for the problems between management and labor! Naturally, existing shareholders, those kindly souls, would never object to having their stock diluted for the benefit of laid-off workers.

Cramer's is only one of the more imaginative (i.e., stupid) schemes floated in recent years to dramatically broaden stock ownership. Stock ownership is still limited almost entirely to the wealthiest 10 or 20 percent of the population, but within this group it's lately become much more evenly distributed. Just as in the 1920s, people who never before owned stocks have been lured into the market by the prospect of 10 percent returns year after year, and their purchases have driven prices still higher, drawing even more *Green*horn investors in behind them.

Behind the aggregate numbers of ever rising stock prices and ever-broadening stock ownership is an interesting pattern: While mutual funds have been massive net buyers, households have been net sellers. In other words, the very rich (the only people who own stocks directly in significant amounts) have been unloading their portfolios on the upper middle class.

Of course, it takes an enormous promotional apparatus to keep the money flowing into those mutual funds and the prices ever-rising. *Green* is just one very small, though strategic, cog in this machinery. Even on its home turf it's overshadowed by much bigger players: Fidelity, whose TV ads hype its appeal to twentysomethings; Morning-star, which packs its cubicles with goateed, nose-ringed mutual fund analysts and newly degreed (but skill-less and experience-less) "consultants"; and brokerages and pension companies like State Street Boston, which lubricate their plots for Social Security privatization with appeals to an imaginary generational conflict in which they, naturally, are on the side of the young. "Excluding senior citizens, there's probably no age group more obsessed with Social Security than post-boomers," write State Street execs Marshall Carter and William Shipman in their 1996 book, *Promises to Keep: Saving Social Security's Dream.* Obsessed in a good way, of course. Brad — a character the authors have made up, but, we're assured, is as typical a Gen-Xer as can be — muses, "Why can't I relieve Social Security — and my fellow taxpayers — of the burden of caring for me in my old age and let me care for myself by letting me save for my own retirement? After all, this is America, isn't it?" To Shipman and Carter — and to *Forbes* magazine, which waxed euphoric over what it called "the most entrepreneurial generation in American history" — Gen Xers seem like a dream come true: They hate Social Security (and their parents and grandparents, who receive it), they love to invest, they're ambitious and hardworking, but "they're not expecting gold watches after spending twenty or more years with one company as dad or grandpa did. Besides, who'd want to?"

All this pales in significance alongside the greatest scheme of them all, the privatization of Social Security. *Green* consistently expresses pessimism about the future existence of Social Security; some of its writers openly call for the program's eradication, while Kurson himself merely presents it as a done deal. Others, like Peterson, Carter and Shipman, are less coy: They make no bones about wanting to junk Social Security in favor of a system of private accounts. Their arguments are motivated by the phenomenal returns on stocks over the past few years. The unmentionable flip side of the last decade's boom, though, is that stocks are now wildly overvalued (whoops! just before press time, it became obvious!). A model developed by Robert Shiller of Yale relates the stock market's average price-earnings ratio over the last ten years to the expected return over the next ten (you can find a lucid summary of Shiller's findings, ornamented with graphs, on the *Left Business Observer* home page). Price-earnings ratios are now well over 25; plugging those numbers into Shiller's formula yields an expected return for the next decade of negative 68 percent. In other words, if historical experience is any guide, the average company's stock is priced at triple what the underlying profits can sustain. For a while, as with any bubble, there are enough suckers to buy overvalued assets at an even higher price to seemingly justify the valuation; but sooner or later you run out of suckers and the bubble bursts.

Dumping the nation's collective retirement account into one of the most overvalued markets since the days of Dutch tulips, though, would neatly bail out the speculators who bought when all the signals said sell. It would also be the scam to end all scams.

No wonder the rich are selling their stocks; they'll soon be buying them back at bargain prices from bankrupt yokels who thought that money would work for just anyone. As they say on the Street, it's during bear markets that money returns to its rightful owners. Dumping Social Security into the stock market will add drama (the numbers will be higher while the fun lasts, and the headache will be much worse afterwards) but it won't change the story in any fundamental way. In the long run, stock prices can grow faster than the economy as a whole only if profits rise at the expense of wages. And economic growth shows no signs of exceeding 2.5 or 3 percent a year, while wages can fall only so far. According to calculations by Dean Baker of the Economic Policy Institute, for 10 percent returns on stocks to continue for the next 40 years, wages would have to fall by a third. Two decades of flat wages have produced Timothy McVeigh and the first major urban riots since the Sixties. Does anyone want to chance what four decades of falling wages would produce? Does anyone — Pete Peterson, Carter and Shipman, Kurson — want to *advocate* it?

Soon, in all likelihood, we will be entering an extended bear market. The privatization of Social Security will be deservedly abandoned. *Green* will be forgotten, as will, hopefully, Peter Peterson. The lambs will have been slaughtered and the money brought back where it belongs. People will find other uses for their spare time and spare cash than playing with stocks, and, most likely, the apologists for capitalism will become a little more circumspect in their praise for unregulated free markets. But only for a while.

In his epic *Feudal Society*, the French historian Marc Bloch describes how in the 16th century, at the very end of the feudal period, when the mounted knight and his personal followers were already long an anachronism, young noblemen could still be found reinventing, apparently from scratch, oaths of allegiance indistinguishable from those used by Charlemagne's vassals 800 years before. Just so, under capitalism, until That Day comes, we shall always have with us the Ken Kursons and the Peter Petersons, naively rediscovering the virtues of *laissez-faire*.

Disorganized Labor
Jacqueline Stewart

STUDIES of African American poverty from the Moynihan Report to the work of sociologist William Julius Wilson have asserted that "when work disappears" from Black urban communities, so does the chastity of teenage girls, the work ethic of young men, and any hope of reversing the downward spiral into the clutches of teen pregnancy, gangs, drugs and violence. High school dropouts, infant mortality, single motherhood, indeed the corrosion of the urban landscape itself, have all been repeatedly attributed to high male unemployment rates in Black communities. The specter of jobless Black men who turn to criminal activity (or worse, leave behind welfare-dependent Black women and children who sap our tax dollars) continues to haunt white people as well as middle-class Blacks who want to reclaim comfortable, cosmopolitan city lifestyles. Black leaders embrace the virtues of work with open arms. Organizers of the 1995 Million Man March purported to refute the negative stereotypes associated with Black men, and yet they seemed to accept the basic premise that lazy Black men who've failed in their roles as husbands and fathers are the real scourge of Black neighborhoods. Minister Louis Farrakhan and others led Black men in ritualistic "atonement" for their sins, telling them to hit the streets and get a job. Plenty of Black women also buy wholeheartedly into fantasies about men in gray flannel suits. Many times I've heard single friends recite their dating mantra: "You've got to have a J-O-B if you want to be with me!"

There are two crucial assumptions behind the onslaught of moralizing about Black work ethics and family values: that a man ought to be at the head of any household, and that work is inherently linked to leadership, morality and inner strength. Now, it's one thing to dream of a man who'll bring home the bacon and wipe your tears away, but when he starts telling you what to buy and what to wear and what to cook for dinner, a lot of my single friends will probably draw the line. But what makes the obsessive focus on returning Black men to work all the more ironic and pathetic is that the kind of work Black men are supposed to do while regaining the "terrible authority" of the father (as Christopher Lasch would put it) is more often than not demeaning, miserable, minimum-wage work. Hardly employment opportunities conducive to building confidence, leadership qualities, or self-respect. In fact, if Black men dared to demonstrate their "leadership" while on the job at the Post Office, they'd be flat out of a job.

Few studies have examined in depth the actual occupational experiences of working-class Black men, and representations of African American men's struggles on the job are rarely featured in the mainstream media. Television shows like *Good Times*, *Roc*, and even the trite new *Cosby* sitcom are among the few programs that have explored work-related issues in Black urban life. The spate of Hollywood "hood" films have also made some superficial observations about inner-city Black men's work experiences. However, a handful of independent African American films, such as Charles Burnett's *Killer of Sheep* (1977) and Billy Woodberry's *Bless Their Little Hearts* (1984), have treated the struggles of working-class Black men with more depth and insight. Actor/director Bill Duke has also been involved in projects that detail working-class Black men's experiences and that challenge the idea of a restored Black patriarchy under a benevolent capitalism. Two films, *The Killing Floor* (1984) and *Car Wash* (1976), deal explicitly with the conflict Black men face working dead-end, low-wage, lousy jobs while striving to be self-sufficient patriarchs. Although these films are not recent, they are perhaps more timely than ever. Merely putting Black men to work, they seem to suggest, is not in itself the solution to restoring their self-image, let alone the salvation of Black families and communities.

These films have received very little critical attention, *The Killing Floor* because it is rarely seen, *Car Wash* because it is rarely taken seriously. They are extremely different in style and tone — *The Killing Floor* has a semi-documentary quality, while *Car Wash* is structured like an anecdotal comedy — and they are set at remote historical moments. Each features three distinct types of Black workers: the un-trustworthy Uncle Tom who kisses up to the white boss and sells out his Black co-workers; the revolutionary, dangerous Black man who refuses to play the game and is ultimately unemployable; and the man in the middle of these extremes, the character who wants to be a good worker and provide for his family but is also painfully aware that he is being exploited and that he must constantly compromise himself on the job. The latter type occupies the central position in both narratives. What is so compelling about *The Killing Floor* and *Car Wash* is that both end on painfully ambivalent notes, suggesting that working-class Black men should attempt to improve their work conditions, but that ultimately they cannot achieve any kind of meaningful

fulfillment on the job or in their personal lives unless larger structural changes take effect.

Languages of Labor

The Killing Floor's Frank Custer (Damien Leake) is a Black man who migrates to Chicago in 1917 and quickly gets caught up in the politics of the stockyard organizing movement. A quasi-historical film based on real-life people and events, *The Killing Floor* features lots of documentary footage of the Chicago stockyards. It also deals with the bloody race riots of the summer of 1919, which serve here as a wake up call for Frank, alerting him to the fact that the union cannot achieve true interracial solidarity, nor can it secure his employment and ability to support his family.

Chicago's meat packing plants circa World War I were nightmarish, bloody, stinking abattoirs. Every morning thousands of workers, the majority of whom were not even citizens, would crowd outside the packinghouse doors; only the "lucky" would be ushered in, to work for fourteen hours amid the stench of blood and offal, while the rest would disappear into nearby saloons. In spite of the terrible conditions, insecure employment and low wages, the packinghouses provided some of the best employment for Black immigrants to Chicago. The packinghouses employed Black workers in skilled positions in a conscious strategy of supporting Black workers so that they would be more loyal to the companies than to their frequently racist white co-workers. Meat packing companies funded Black philanthropies, paid for anti-union lectures, and set up hiring halls in the middle of Black neighborhoods whenever there was a strike. The packers carefully appealed to Black men's desires for individual self-advancement, precisely in order to manipulate the hatred of the white

most part, have failed to challenge this myth, choosing instead to uphold traditional notions of self-sufficiency and male-dominated families. But, as these films assert, when working-class Black men buy into the ideals of patriarchy and individualism, they act to benefit their bosses — not themselves — and they ultimately remain frustrated and disappointed with their lives. Both Lonnie and Frank work to support their families, but the fate of their more radical friends only shows them how trapped they really are. The myriad oppressions they have inherited cannot be surmounted simply by working hard at one's job. Sure, African American communities need good, well-paid jobs, but they also need new housing, better schools, affordable health care, and real political representation. Providing "legitimate" employment for Black men will not, in itself, lead to the magical restoration of Black communities. But still we march along, led by Daniel Patrick Moynihan and with Minister Farrakhan bringing up the rear, blithely ignoring the fact of exploitation, and condemning the inner city to even further corrosion.

Why Johnny Can't Organize
Bob Fitch

O N the dust jacket of his book, *America Needs A Raise*, recently elected AFL-CIO President John J. Sweeney compares his first months in office to FDR's celebrated 100 days. Certainly, like Roosevelt, he's been driving the Republicans crazy. In the fall '96 campaign, the *Wall Street Journal* estimated that labor's spending for congressional and presidential races more than tripled its previous high, topping $50 million. And Sweeney pledged $20 million more for organizing drives; his "Union Summer" campaign put 1,500 students from elite college campuses in the field; he's supervised a new outreach from the Federation to minorities and women; he's replaced Cold Warriors with radicals in upper-echelon staff jobs. Sweeney even joined the Democratic Socialists of America.

But is this renewal for real? There have been turnaround efforts before: The 1970 purging of the Teamsters was supposed to show how serious labor was about getting rid of institutional corruption, just as letting them back in unreformed in 1980 demonstrated labor's new no-nonsense pragmatism. In 1986, the federation presided over a stunningly frank analysis of the labor movement's weaknesses accompanied by a program for renewal. The program was never implemented.

A decade later, it's not too cynical to ask whether this is a comeback of George Foreman proportions or whether we're just witnessing another of organized labor's Judy Garlandesque recoveries — a temporary gathering of resolve, accompanied by rave reviews, only to be followed by the inevitable relapse. What makes the question so crucial is the spreading recognition that what's pushed America so far to the right, and made the United States the country with the greatest income inequalities and crummiest welfare state in the OECD, is nothing other than advanced capitalism's feeblest labor movement. At the same time, we owe labor plenty. What we still have in the way of public education, pensions, public assistance, and the eight-hour day were things that organized labor delivered. It matters terribly if we have terrible unions.

So how *is* Sweeney doing? The politic stance would be to declare that it's too soon to tell. The strength and significance of unions can't be measured by the number of people paying dues. Still, it tells you something if organized labor can't organize anyone.

The latest, unpublished figures from the National Labor Relations Board suggest that little has changed to arrest labor's slow march to extinction. In the first nine months of Sweeney's tenure, the number of organizing wins fell to an all-time low. So did the number of victories as a percentage of total elections. As a result, the share of workers who are union members fell another half percent — to 14.5. And the number of private-sector union members actually fell to below 10 million. It was 17 million in 1970, when there were more than 30 percent fewer private sector workers.

Richard Rothstein, a careful student of labor organizing and supporter of the new organizing focus, cautions in the *American Prospect* that labor needs to triple the number of workers it organizes to reach a 15 percent share sometime in the early 2010s.

Given the magnitude of the task, what's striking is not how much money

presents a more subtle representation of Black men's experiences on the job. Although *Car Wash* is probably best known for its soundtrack (particularly its disco theme song performed by Rose Royce), it also offers one of the very few, and very best, cinematic representations of working-class African American men. The comic premise of *Car Wash* turns upon a popular, long-standing stereotype about African American men — that they have no "work ethic."

Car Wash features a multiracial cast of characters who work at and patronize a Los Angeles car wash. The film goes to great pains to represent a full working day in detail — the workers arriving at the car wash, changing into their work clothes, washing cars and dealing with customers, engaging in lunch hour antics, washing more cars, changing back into their street clothes, closing up and finally heading home. The panorama of personalities who work at the car wash (about 16 cast members) spend as much time goofing off as washing cars, demonstrating constantly that this is a job they cannot take seriously for very long. Their work environment is chaotic and infantalizing; at various moments the boss has to remind them that they are at work, not on a playground.

Although *Car Wash* is usually considered a superficial, Blaxploitation-era comedy, the film's humor has a double edge, demonstrating the variety of techniques the characters employ to overcome the frustrating, exploitative nature of their dead-end jobs. The cast includes a variety of eccentric personalities, including Sly (Garrett Morris), a con artist who takes bets on baseball and horse races; Lindy (Antonio Fargas), a wisecracking transvestite diva; and Floyd and Lloyd (Darrow Igus and DeWayne Jessie), a duo who spend the day rehearsing their R & B act. Although these characters may seem foolish, it becomes clear that their preoccupations with various individual styles (hair, clothes, side jobs, hobbies, etc.) are more than mere attempts to express their individual identities; they try to distance themselves from the menial work that they perform. For example, Tall Chief (Henry Kingi), the Native American car washer, wears a pig-ear hat that he refuses to remove. T. C. (Franklyn Ajaye) wears a T-shirt emblazoned with his self-designed alter-ego/superhero character, "The Fly," and occasionally "buzzes" at his enemies. The seductive yet ultimately futile individualism in *The Killing Floor* appears to be a new mode of rebellion in *Car Wash*. T-shirts, slick dance moves and jokes appear to have taken the place of organization. After all, who needs a union when you have a pig-ear hat?

The workers in *Car Wash* mock the notion of organized labor through their antics on the job. Irwin (Richard Brestoff), son of the owner, Mr. Bernstein (Sully Boyer), is an annoying college student who quotes Mao and spends the day trying to bond with the disinterested workers. Instead of using his college education to help his father with the bookkeeping, Irwin smokes pot in the men's room and proclaims, "I want to be one of the working class. Workers of the world unite!" The working men's response is to run an unsuspecting Irwin through the car wash, dousing him with soap and water.

Having dismissed Irwin and his shallow communist shtick, the film offers a more appropriate leader. Lonnie (Ivan Dixon), a middle-aged African American man, is by far the car wash's most diligent employee. An ex-con, Lonnie must work extremely hard to keep his job and support his wife and two children. He's the first character to arrive at work, and we learn that Mr. Bernstein, or Mr. B, gives him extra cash for opening and closing shop. Throughout the film, Lonnie's seriousness contrasts with the behavior of the other workers, who spend the day playing pranks and spraying each other with cleaning fluids.

Although Lonnie clearly stands apart from the other workers, he does not claim superiority over them, as does Earl (Leonard Jackson), the sell-out of the crew who avoids all hard, unpleasant labor. Earl appears to have some seniority in the car wash, and he assumes a managerial attitude toward the other workers. Earl refuses to get wet, and spends the day offering special detailing services to affluent white customers for big tips. At the film's end, Earl is humiliated by the other workers, who place a pile of dog shit, which Earl had refused to clean up earlier, on the hood of his car. Not quite as malicious as Heavy, the compromised Black worker in *The Killing Floor*, Earl is nonetheless disrespected by his fellow workers and parodied by the film itself.

On the other end of the spectrum is Abdullah (played by none other than Bill Duke, the director of *The Killing Floor*), the Black militant character. The other workers ridicule Abdullah's embrace of Islam and a Black Nationalism and continue to call him by his given name, Duane. Abdullah has lost tolerance for his "slave job," and walks through the film with a chip on his shoulder and a disgusted expression on his face. At the end of the day, Mr. B fires him.

Lonnie sympathizes with Abdullah, but the precariousness of Lonnie's position as middle man becomes evident when he tries to talk to Mr. B on Abdullah's behalf. Mr. B is too frustrated to listen to Lonnie's arguments. He also refuses to discuss Lonnie's request for a raise and his ideas about how to make the car wash more profitable. Lonnie's attempts to distinguish himself on the job appear to have largely been in vain.

Lonnie has a great deal invested in his job; not only must he fulfill his parole conditions, but he must also financially support his family and maintain his dependents' respect for him as the hardworking head of his household. At one point, Lonnie's son and daughter visit him on the job and his daughter presents him with a crayon drawing of him working at the car wash. At this highly sentimental moment, the film seems to support the notion that as long as a man like Lonnie works hard, he can overcome the troubles he faces and succeed. Indeed, after their talk, Mr. B finds Lonnie in the locker room and earnestly promises to have a serious discussion with Lonnie about everything on his mind.

Just when it seems that *Car Wash* works out the tensions between a Black working-class man and his white employer a little too neatly, a crucial complication arises. After closing, Abdullah returns to the car wash with a gun as Lonnie is counting up the day's cash. Abdullah accuses Lonnie of being too concerned with protecting Mr. B's property, and threatens to shoot him and steal the money. After a few tense moments, Lonnie convinces Abdullah to hand over the gun. Abdullah begins to cry on Lonnie's shoulder, repeating, "Everything's falling apart."

Here the film recognizes that the pressures that have pushed Abdullah to such extremes are felt by other Black men as well (both within and outside of the film), whether or not they possess the language to express it. When Abdullah says that he can't stand the "clown show" atmosphere of the car wash, he is explaining the film's comedic pretense. The workers' games, jokes, and slacking, now appear as stubborn, if finally ineffectual, attempts to maintain their individuality, disguising the deeper frustrations they share about being trapped on the job at the car wash, prisoners of the workplace.

Like the workers in *Car Wash*, many struggling inner-city African Americans still cling to the false promise of the American Dream. Black leaders, for the

workers and sabotage any attempts to organize.

The Killing Floor chronicles Frank's deepening participation in such an attempt, one which ends in disillusionment and failure. The film contrasts Frank's work within the union to his work within the plant to show that his labor in both these institutions is not enough to change his situation.

Frank's changing relationship to language serves as a metaphor for his deepening involvement in the union. On his first day on the job — mopping blood from the cutting room floor — Frank hears many languages as Slavs and Poles work side by side with African Americans. Frank's initial reaction is confusion: "How was you supposed to work with folks you couldn't understand none?" But at Frank's first visit to a union meeting, he learns that there are some words all workers understand. Here speeches are delivered in Eastern European languages, and then translated into English. All around him, white men and women work themselves up into a frenzy, alternately cheering in their native languages and chanting "Union!" Their enthusiasm reminds Frank of prayer meetings back down South, and he comes to feel a solidarity with his co-workers across racial and cultural lines as he observes them "testifying," "getting happy" and "speaking in tongues." Eventually, Frank enters into the multi-lingual family of the union.

The union meeting is one of several moments in *The Killing Floor* in which the transformative power of language is emphasized. Early in the film Frank seeks out the services of a "professional" letter writer, Miss Lila (Mary Alice), to whom he dictates correspondence to his wife back home in the South. During their first meeting, Miss Lila consistently alters Frank's words, transforming his crude, matter-of-fact phrases into florid, descriptive prose.

After a while, Frank begins to assert his own personality more and more, and he insists that she write his letters as he dictates them.

Miss Lila encourages Frank to join the union, and slowly he rises to a leadership position. Union leaders assign him the task of convincing skeptical Black workers to cross the formidable color line and join the union. Frank must learn how to translate union rhetoric (which is coded as "white") into a language his Black co-workers can understand and embrace. As Frank grows into his new position as a Black union organizer, he is transformed from someone who needs translators to someone who can perform his own translations and speak in his own voice. Union membership betokens individual development; Frank's work in the union lends him dignity, self-respect, his own language, his own powerful voice.

As Frank gets more involved in the labor movement, he is challenged at every turn by resentful white bosses and fearful Black co-workers. Frank's biggest Black enemy is Austin "Heavy" Williams (Moses Gunn), a middle-aged worker who is being paid off by the stockyard bosses to create racial tension and prevent Blacks from joining the union. Heavy repeatedly tells Frank that the white union members could never be his "brothers." But while Heavy may be a unionbusting troublemaker, during the riots his words begin to ring true. Roving white mobs prevent Black workers from walking safely to their jobs, causing them to lose weeks of wages. In one scene, a group of Black men gather at a community center to pick up food baskets provided by the stockyard bosses. As Black workers' families suffer, white union members seem to be doing nothing to help. "Where are your brothers now?" Heavy asks, and Frank has no answer. One after another, Frank's Black recruits turn in their union buttons.

Frank's belief in interracial union

organization is also challenged by his childhood friend, Thomas Joshua (Ernest Rayford). Thomas and Frank migrated to Chicago together, but their lives take very different directions. On his first day working at the stockyards, Thomas is beat up by a group of white men. Labeled a "smart mouthed nigger," Thomas decides to join the army rather than put up with hellish packinghouse labor and the taunts and insults of racist co-workers. When he returns to Chicago after serving in World War I, Thomas is unable to find work — even at the stockyards. His inability to get a job and the disrespect he constantly encounters despite his military service leads him to join a group of armed, radical Blacks during the riots. Frank refuses Thomas's offer to retaliate against white violence, and soon after learns that Thomas has been killed.

Frank's disillusionment following Thomas's death reflects how difficult it is for Black urban working-class men, then and now, to maintain their jobs and their self respect at the same time. Their options are dismal: They must either turn their backs on each other and their white co-workers, risk losing their jobs if they unionize or endanger their lives if they try to buck the system altogether. At many moments *The Killing Floor* comes across as a vehemently pro-union film. The fervor of the union meetings and the portrayal of white union men as color-blind good guys suggests that an interracial alliance might have been formed. And in the 1930s, the CIO was able to organize the packinghouses by explicitly appealing to Black workers, using Black organizations to build the union. But in his individual labor — either in the union or the packing plant — Frank cannot maintain his dignity. He cannot change the consciousness of his community or even ensure his family's subsistence. In the end, Frank does get his job back, but as a scab. He pins on his union button, but on the inside of his shirt — driving his political beliefs underground until they can safely re-emerge, through other voices, decades later.

Labor and Style

WHILE *The Killing Floor* offers an extremely pessimistic view of the Black laborer's position, *Car Wash,*

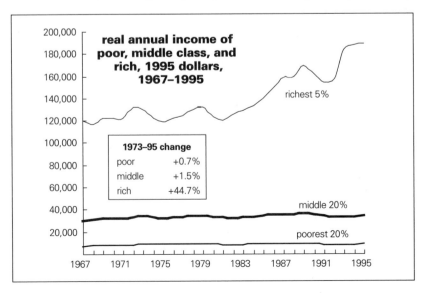

real annual income of poor, middle class, and rich, 1995 dollars, 1967–1995

richest 5%

1973–95 change	
poor	+0.7%
middle	+1.5%
rich	+44.7%

middle 20%

poorest 20%

1967   1971   1975   1979   1983   1987   1991   1995

labor is devoting to organizing, but how little. Unions may be member poor, but they're asset rich. Every year AFL-CIO unions take in $6 billion. Consider also that the $20 million Sweeney plans to spend on organizing is to cover two years. And that Sweeney announced recently the federation was spending $150 million on a real estate project in San Francisco.

The yawning gap between labor's means and its ends raises fundamental questions about how seriously the AFL-CIO leaders take the problem of their disappearing membership. It strikes to the heart of the question of American unions' identity, and the reasons why they don't act like unions in other advanced capitalist countries.

Can anyone imagine what took place in France in December 1995 — when public-sector workers closed down the country in the fight against austerity — happening here? Can you close your eyes and envision the French scenario happening in a single city? "Well, that's the French," you might say. "They have a revolutionary tradition."

But in October 1995, Canadian workers were able to present a solid front that nearly shut down Toronto. That same month, 475,000 German metal workers protested sick-pay cuts. And in Israel, last summer's protest against the Likud's plan for shrinking family child allowances mobilized 500,000 workers in protest (the equivalent of 35 million in the United States). Recall, by contrast, that when Clinton signed the welfare bill last summer, Sweeney sent a telegram.

Our unions act differently from European unions because they are institutionally different. In France — as in Italy and Spain — three main federations, corresponding to the three major political tendencies on the left — compete for members. In northern Europe and Scandinavia, unions sit on corporate boards. And they control labor parties that even in opposition can veto government policy.

What distinguishes American unions from unions elsewhere is not just that they don't have a labor party. It's not just their weak leverage in a weak state. What really marks them is their peculiar localistic character.

But what's wrong with local unionism? Won't local leaders be closer to members than remote bureaucrats off in some D.C. headquarters? Maybe, but at the same time, American unions have not only the most highly paid leaders, but the most staff, and the most highly paid staffs in the world.

These bloated staffs don't make American unions "bureaucratic." To be bureaucratic requires centralization, the power to administer a law or a contract. The fragmentation and competitive relations between American unions makes real bureaucratic administration impossible. The staff people aren't true bureaucrats. They constitute a kind of patronage machine.

American unions — especially the crafts, but also Teamsters, Hotel Workers, Laborers — are a lot like the dying urban Democratic Party machines they support. Race and ethnicity provide the glue for boss-client relations. At best, leaders provide services for members rather than allow democratic participation in the life of the union. Moreover, it's the self-perpetuating local character of American monopoly unions that makes them so uniquely weak, corrupt, and undemocratic. It's the same localism that explains the continued and largely undiscussed exclusion of non-whites and women from the construction trades.

America is a big country that's never been organized. We've always had a core of craft and locally based unions like the Teamsters. But even in the 1930s, we never fully reached the stage of national bargaining. The UAW and the Steelworkers stopped at the Mason-Dixon line.

What the CIO achieved — opposed mightily by the AFL, remember — was the 1935 Wagner Act, which provides American workers with the only rights they have against employers. But the Wagner Act gives workers precious little leverage against their union leaders. Unlike other countries, where workers can choose what union to join, in America workers have no alternative.

In states with closed-shop laws, the union is the workers' exclusive bargaining representative. You don't have to join. But you must pay dues. Power over workers is especially great in unions where there is a hiring hall. The union can determine whether a worker works or not. Dissidents don't work.

In the United States, the existence of the AFL-CIO as a national coordinating body obscures the localistic character of American unions. The AFL-CIO's president has extremely limited power over the member unions. Think of Kofi Annan in relation to the heads of states of members

of the United Nations and you begin to get an idea of the scope of his powers.

There is no national bargaining going on among the individual craft unions. Each union bargains within its local jurisdictional franchise. Last summer in New York, construction unions bargained with contractors in a fragmented way — bricklayers, carpenters, painters, and sheet metal workers each signed separate agreements. And the same is true of city workers: teachers, cops, firemen, and transit workers, all bargain individually. Even the Auto Workers, Steelworkers, and Rubber Workers unions, which came closest to the European social-democracy model of national unions, have lost their power to carry out pattern bargaining.

To see why localism works this way, consider an urban construction local — say, the New York City Carpenters, with 19,000 dues-paying members. Look at

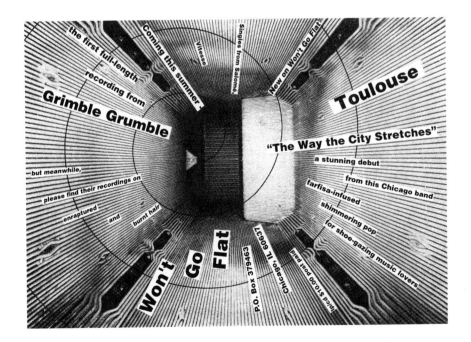

```
*OBITUARY*
ANNIE BYRNE DIES, ALONE AND
NEVER MARRIED, AT THE AGE OF 75.
```

Dear Miss Byrne:

A fictitious obituary? Perhaps.

But when it comes to finding a husband, the facts are grim:
   *There are over 150,000 single women in New York City
      Murphy Brown ratings are at an all-time high.
      This town is crawling with competition.
   *30% of the men deemed "eligible" by most surveys are
   actually prisoners. And fewer than 1/3 of those prisoners
   are serving sentences for white-collar crimes.
   *Pretty much everyone who's really fun is gay.

The fact is, there just aren't that many good men out there.

HOW MANY MORE NIGHTS CAN YOU SIT AT HOME ALONE WATCHING MARY
TYLER MOORE ON NICK AT NIGHT AND EATING MOO SHU VEGETABLES?

You can't do it anymore, **Annie**, can you?

That's why I'm writing to you — to ask you to marry me. Please
affix the YES sticker to the attached envelope send the enclosed
envelope with your answer today.

A legal marriage with me will protect you from the stigma of
being a lonely old maid 24 hours a day, 7 days a week, anywhere in
the world.

What is peace of mind like that worth these days?

Please marry me, Annie, before another gray hair appears on
your head. **I've extended this unbelievable offer until October
15, 1996.** Mail your response today. Thank you.

Sincerely Yours,
Richie Glickman
Customer Service Representative
Omni American Card
```
```

Dear Ms Byrne:

Recently, I invited you to be my bride. My reason was clear.

As a highly valued female cardmember, you <u>deserve</u> to join the select group of women who enter into matrimony.

Being married to me instantly identifies you as someone special. You'll enjoy a new degree of respect and attention from waitresses who formerly sneered, "Table for one?" at you or acted sympathetic which was even worse. You'll be instantly upgraded at hotels across the United States and around the world. You'll even be invited to more dinner parties.

The portfolio of benefits offered to you by marrying me will noticeably augment those you currently enjoy and will enhance the way you lead your life.

Complimentary Companion Tickets to My Parents' Home In Minneapolis, Minnesota Every Thanksgiving

With married life comes the joy of an extended family. "Mom" and "Dad" Glickman will welcome you every Thanksgiving with a home cooked meal, including yams, turkey and traditional stuffing, all with no salt added.

A Night Table For Your Side Of The Bed

You will be entitled to a walnut night table to fill with photograph albums, bedtime reading and maybe even, God willing, baby books.

Safe Sex

You'll receive a signed certificate, suitable for framing, from a qualified medical practitioner, ensuring that I am free from all sexually transmittable diseases — *a valuable thing to know in this day and age.*

It's O.K., I Was Up.®,
My Exclusive 24-Hour Listening Service

Whether you have a bad dream, or you're lying awake seething with rage over the way I leave my socks on the living room floor, or you're up at 4 a.m. convincing yourself you have cancer, you can wake me up and I'll listen. Really listen.

You've earned this recognition and now I believe you should be wearing the ring that signifies your value: my wedding ring.

Sincerely,
Richie Glickman
Customer Service Representative
Omni American Card

   P.S. If you have already responded to my offer, please excuse this reminder letter. I just wanted to be sure you were aware of this very special offer.

Dear Miss Byrne:

Just what the hell were you doing spending $156 at **The Odeon** and $128 for tickets to *Rent* last Thursday?

Never mind how I know.

I hope you haven't started dating. I've enclosed a brochure on the risks of rape, disease, attack and scam artistry. It's just plain stupid.

I want you. I want to marry you. <u>I know we're perfect for each other</u> .

It's not too late to respond.

Look. Meet me.

Let me help resolve whatever it is that's keeping you away. Simply bring this letter to my apartment at 190 Waverly Place #4B and redeem it for a FREE DINNER AT LA GRENOUILLE **worth well over $156,** you may rest assured.

Don't spend another night, or another cent, with some cheapskate loser you picked up God Knows Where.

Come over now and I'll never mention this little date of yours ever again, I swear.

Do we have a deal?

I look forward to seeing you.

Sincerely,
Richie Glickman
Customer Service Representative
Omni American Card

Direct Male

Risa Mickenberg

A private message to a special friend.

Dear Annie Byrne:

This is a private invitation sent to you alone. I hope you'll accept my proposal. But even if you decide not to, I want to send you a gift....**ABSOLUTELY FREE**.

Yes. A 4 1/4" x 4 3/4" table-top calculator (battery included) — with a wide display screen and large keys will be delivered right to your door. You can't buy this fabulous calculator at any store in **New York**. But it can be yours...without any obligation...simply by saying you'd like to have it!

Why I'm Writing To You

The list from which I selected your name indicates that you are a single, 34-year-old woman who earns $90,575, is concerned with fashion and health, has a cursory knowledge of politics, a bit of a Barney's addiction and a penchant for a certain discreet sex toy mail order catalog.

I like your profile.

I want you to marry me and as a FREE GIFT to you, Annie, you will receive the **marvelous table top calculator**.

How can I make such an incredible offer?

As Customer Service Representative for the Omni American Card, I see millions of interesting women in our database, but none whose spending habits and psychographic profile excite me the way yours do.

I'm confident that you will enjoy my sense of humor. My endearing mannerisms. My dog. **My full head of blonde hair**. You'll get it all when you marry me by **September 16, 1996**.

I'm sure you'll be delighted and intrigued by every little thing I do, Annie. Won't you accept this free calculator and be my wife?

Sincerely,
Richie Glickman
Customer Service Representative
Omni American Card

P.S. This **FREE GIFT** offer expires after August 16, 1996. I urge you to return it today.

the local from the standpoint of the leadership. Forget the cash that comes from managing pension funds, health funds, vacation funds, etc., and just look at the income that comes from dues: 3 percent dues on $50,000 a year per worker. That's $28.5 million to spread around.

How do the leaders make sure that cash flow continues? By organizing the unorganized? That might bring in more dues. But work is scarce. And as we've seen, creating more slots for apprentices means less work for those already waiting in the hiring hall.

Then, too, there's the politics of the local monopoly. Self-perpetuating political machines don't strive for the highest turnout. They strive to get *their* people to cast ballots. Union machines work similarly. They rely on those whom they've given staff jobs. The New York carpenters employ nearly 300 people just in managing their various funds. These individuals can be counted on.

Only somewhat less reliable are the workers who get sent out on jobs from the hiring hall. Essentially, union members are clients of business agent bosses. A change in business agents might mean a change in who gets to work. Thus for staff workers and leaders alike, bringing in new members upsets the electoral status quo. That's why, for example, there are vanishingly few non-white carpenters in the Bronx although the Bronx is overwhelmingly non-white.

Of course, the most secure union leader is the one who suppresses voting altogether. Elections in American unions rarely exist at all above the local level. In the handful of unions where members do elect national officers, it is usually because of a Justice Department consent decree — as in the Teamsters and Laborers Union.

The goal of the leadership is *unaccountability*. And they succeed in meeting this goal well over 90 percent of the time. Of course, not being accountable to anyone doesn't promote democracy, honesty, or true organizational strength. Our unions substitute staff for member participation; a narrow pursuit of local self-interest replaces broader solidarity;

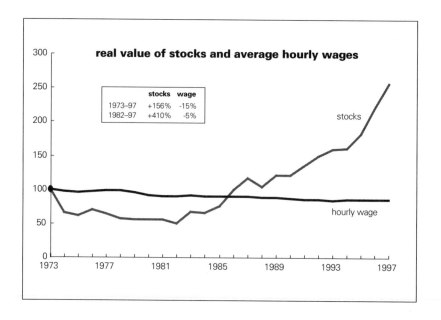

real value of stocks and average hourly wages

	stocks	wage
1973–97	+156%	-15%
1982–97	+410%	-5%

a corrupt boss-client system replaces socialist perspectives.

Privately, many "friends of labor" will concede that the construction unions are corrupt. "But that's really a minority of all the unions," they point out. Actually, at the crucial local level, the construction unions aren't a minority. They dominate central labor councils across the country. And what does it say when the big political campaign mounted this year by New York's Central Labor Council is not to defend tenants, but *landlords* in their effort to strip three million apartment dwellers of rent protection; not to protect their own members against the mayor's plan to replace them with 135,000 people who would work only for welfare checks, but to defeat legislation aimed at at removing mob-connected union leaders who control produce markets.

Leftists frequently insist we shouldn't mention union corruption. Aren't the bosses more corrupt? Why not focus on corporate crime? Certainly it's greater in dollar terms. But bosses' corruption comes at stockholders' expense. Union corruption comes at the expense of members. More fundamentally, corruption reinforces the separation between the members and the leaders, especially since corruption can't be understood simply as a matter of personal lapses. Frequently it's the aim of office.

It's difficult to quantify the corruption of labor leaders. But sometimes the brazenness involved can be revealing, especially since the leaders are already so overpaid. The head of the French CGT makes the equivalent of $29,000. Edward Devine, until a few months ago the head of the carpenters union in New York City, made $350,000. And after the Justice Department forced him out of office, he stole paintings from the walls of headquarters. Recently, the world's largest collection of Joyceana — personal effects of James Joyce — went on sale at an auction house in New York. The seller? Bernard Silverman, formerly of Teamster's Local 858. Mr. Silverman needed cash after being forced to leave office by the Justice Department.

Unions define their problems in external terms. They lack members because of bad labor laws, Republicans in Congress, employer hostility, union-busting lawyers. All true. But how can millions of members be mobilized to combat these forces? Especially when their leaders' survival depends on machines designed to transform them into passive consumers of union services.

Our peculiar local monopoly, boss-client system — which reminds one more of European feudalism than European social democracy — is what constitutes the true obstacle to organizing. Patronage, racial exclusion, lack of democracy and corrupt practices don't constitute abuses of the system. They *are* the system. Nor is the rest of the Left — academics, journalists, staffers, "friends of labor" — entirely innocent. By keeping silent on the internal sources of labor's decline, focusing only on the approved external sources, and ignoring the fight for union democracy, progressives trade off the truth for institutional access, consulting contracts, staff jobs, speaking engagements, and organizing grants.

In this century, the great gains made by American labor have never been achieved by following the strategies of the mainline federation leaders — the Lane Kirklands, George Meanys, and William Greens. Initially, the AFL even opposed the Wagner Act. What's always made the difference in workers' lives has been mass organizing, factory occupations, sitdown strikes, a war of maneuver. Not the protracted war of position envisioned by Sweeney. Who will win a contest between capital and labor where the battlefield is the NLRB, the courts, and the Congress, in which the contestants are professional staffs, and the primary resource is cash? It is, unfortunately, not too soon to tell. ❧

DID I DO SOMETHING WRONG?

Dear Annie:

I haven't received your response.
I've sent you several notices, asking for your hand in
marriage but I haven't received your answer.
Please take the time to fill out the response card and
mail it back today. At this point, we'll be lucky if we
can find a halfway decent place for the reception.

Cordially,
Richie Glickman
Customer Service Representative
Omni American Card

Dear Miss Byrne:

You've moved!

It's a busy time. New apartment, lots of unpacking to
do, a bunch of light switches to figure out, a whole new
life. You were probably too busy to send a simple change of
address, right?

Don't apologize.
It's fine.

Chances are, when the craziness dies down and you're
lying in that empty apartment, surrounded by empty boxes and
wads of packing tape, you'll wish you had someone — at least
to help you reach those high shelves.

This is just a reminder that wherever you go, in every
state and in 52 countries, whenever you need me, I am here.
I can find you and be there in twelve hours.

Whether you need medical attention, a cash advance or
you're finally ready to make a commitment that will provide
you with the love, honor and respect you deserve, I'll
always be here. 24 hours a day. A phone call away.
Whenever you're ready. I will find you.

I look forward to hearing from you.

Sincerely,
Richie Glickman
Customer Service Representative
Omni American Card

REMAINDER TABLE

ROBERT NEDELKOFF

The Invisible Novelist

S ITTING to the right of my keyboard as I write are a book and a magazine. The book, purchased for ten cents at the (Salinas, California) John Steinbeck (public) Library's discard shelf, is a dog-eared copy of the very first of the fifty or so books about Thomas Pynchon, written by Joseph W. Slade and published as the last of Warner Paperback Library's "Writers for the Seventies" series in December 1974. The cover shows a bearded man's head, photographed from the back. In a Ninuties reissue of the book, Slade informed the reader that the head was his own, not Pynchon's; the publisher, apparently, thought that the most recent photo of Pynchon then known to exist, from his 1953 Cornell University student register, wouldn't quite cut it. The blurb page asks who, exactly, is "this shadowy, enigmatic figure who refuses to be interviewed or photographed. . . ?"

I put the book aside and open the November 11, 1996 issue of *New York*, to page 61. Therein is reproduced a photo of a man, seen from the back, walking down a street in the West Seventies of Manhattan, his small son by his side. The man carries a canvas totebag strapped across one shoulder, wears an oilcloth jacket, and sports a hat similar to the one Don Novello wears in his Father Guido Sarducci persona. The long gray hair curling over the collar of the jacket reinforces the Sarducci resemblance. The caption informs us that this man is Thomas Pynchon. The text of the article goes on to confirm what has already become common knowledge among the Pynchon cultists: that the man, for about all of this decade, has lived much the same life in Manhattan as any moderately successful, Macarthur-winning writer — going to dinner parties, chatting with Susan Sontag, lunching with Don De Lillo, going to the Hamptons or Westchester County every now and then. At article's end, when Steve Erickson informs *Cups* magazine that Pynchon is mulling the idea of a signing tour to promote his new novel *Mason & Dixon*, the "news" is thoroughly anticlimactic. A literary agent, more on the ball

than most of his kind, notes: "The people who are into Pynchon wouldn't want to see him in person." Indeed, when one opens *Details* and finds that Jessica Kaplan — the precocious seventeen-year-old who is Michael Stipe's favorite screenwriter and Oliver Stone's favorite director (before she's even directed yet) — believes that one's pal Francesca Lia Block is "the first writer since Pynchon to remake the language," one is startled to find that any teenager, most likely to have encountered Pynchon through *Vineland*, or maybe his liner notes to Lotion's *Nobody's Cool*, could want to investigate him further. Sure, when I was Jessica's age, back when Slade's book came out, I thought Pynchon was God. But he had not written the liner notes to, say, Left End's *Spoiled Rotten*.

At this point, the only thing Pynchon could do that would raise an eyebrow is get resolutely downmarket — like (assuming he does follow through on what he said to Erickson) limiting his book signings to Super Crown stores only. Forget the suggestion of a publicist in the *New York* article that he do bookchat on *60 Minutes, 20/20, Fresh Air* — it would have to be what he could get from the Big Five.

Let's start with the man who beat Letterman with the Dancing Itos:

> **Pynchon:** *... Now, back when I still lived in California, in Aptos up by Santa Cruz, I had this 1963 Buick Skylark — this would have been around 1978 — and the way I'd keep sand from blowing under the hood and getting into the air filter was to coat the filter with mink oil a little. No friction at all — the sand would slide right off.*
>
> **Jay:** *Really? Somebody told me Mazola did the trick, but I dunno. Now, you've just written this book here, Mason & Dixon, and man, this is a big one! A regular doorstop. How long is it?*
>
> **Pynchon:** *Um, about 700 pages.*
>
> **Jay:** *Really? What's it about?*
>
> **Pynchon:** *Well, it's about the guys who laid out the Mason and Dixon line that divides the North and South.*

Jay: So it's about the Civil War, like *Gone With The Wind.*
Liv Tyler: Wasn't *Gone With The Wind* a book as well as a movie?
Pynchon: I think so.
Liv: It was like, they put out a book with the movie, based on the script. It was, like, a novelization. My mom used to have it when I was a kid.
Pynchon: Well, I think that —
Jay: Back to your book, Tom. Now, does Lincoln show up in this? Lincoln was some President, eh, folks? No Big Macs for him...

Now, to the Hoosier himself:

Dave: I'm telling you, Tom, this is some book! Look at this thing, Paul. How big did you say this was, Tom?
Pynchon: About 700 pages.
Dave: That's a lot of pages, Tom. It's more like a beach read. Any reason for putting it out right now, in March?
Pynchon: Beach read — how do you mean —
David Spade: Irony, Tom, it's a concept — over and above, get my drift?
Pynchon: Well, I —
Dave: Not to change the subject here, but weren't you on "The John Laroquette Show" awhile back, Tom?
Pynchon: Not exactly, I was the subject of —
Dave, in his version of a Cajun accent: Ah'm aw Weezeeawnuh Maahn!
(Cheers, applause)

A stopover with a Harvard man:

Conan: Now, Tom, you were around back in the Sixties. The Sixties were something else, weren't they?
Pynchon: They sure were.
Conan: One of my writers told me he heard you used to date Joan Baez back then.
Pynchon: I'd rather not talk about —
Conan: I dunno, Tom. She looked OK with that long hair back then, but after she cut it short and kind of let it go gray, she really started looking sexy to me. I don't know — it might be the Irish in me —
Andy: I used to be Chinese, myself.
Conan: Oh, Andy, you're such a kidder.
Tori Spelling: Joan Baez — wasn't she a singer like Pat Benatar? I want to play Pat Benatar in, like, a made-for-TV movie. She had a really dramatic life.
Pynchon: Pat Benatar, I believe, named an album —

Conan: Speaking of albums, Tom, didn't you write the liner notes to Lotion's last one? We had Lotion on our show. Great guys.
Andy: I had them for breakfast. They were very good with blueberry syrup.
Conan: Oh, Andy ...

Well, let's just skip Tom (as in Snyder) and Larry. Not to be skipped, of course, would be Pynchon's spot on another show:

Pynchon: ...no friction at all — the sand would slide right off.
RuPaul: Well, Tom, when I was selling Porsches down in Atlanta, I heard from people who took them down to Myrtle Beach that Brylcreem on the filter was really what would keep the sand out.
Bill: I hate to interrupt, guys, but this show is about politics, not cars. Big topic tonight: Tabitha is getting hitched to that hunky neoliberal Michael Lewis. Your take, Jenny?
Jenny McCarthy: Well excuuuuse me (grimaces) but I think (grimace, jiggle) that Tabitha's dude (sneers) is no hunk (grimace). He's got flab, flab, flab (sneer, jiggle).
James Carville: Ah'm a Luzianne Maan!
RuPaul: I'm curious, Bill. Usually the panel here consists of two people in politics and two people from other areas. Tonight we seem to have just one politician.
Bill: No, we have two. Tom here founded the SDS, right?
Pynchon: Um, not exactly . . . .

But the point of all this is simply that Thomas Pynchon long since has ceased to be an underground man in the world of American letters. He is part of the mainstream. This article concerns a man who, if still alive, is genuinely "out there."

To the left of my keyboard is a book I bought for a quarter from the same discard shelf: *Shake It For the World, Smartass* by Seymour Krim. Krim, of course, was the man who functioned as an intermediary between the mainstream literary world and the Beats — that is, when he wasn't grappling with his bipolar illness (as described in his essay "The Insanity Bit"). This book was the follow-up to his "underground classic" *Views of a Nearsighted Cannoneer*. Krim killed himself in 1989 and a book of his selected essays, put together by James Wolcott, was issued later.

After buying it, I went home and looked through the chapters at random. The book consisted of looks at Krim's usual mix of subjects: profiles of Dave McReynolds (of the War Resisters' League) and Jan Cremer, both names very big in the Sixties and half-forgotten now; reviews, sometimes expanded from their original publication, of books by Nelson Algren, Leslie Fiedler, Paul Goodman. (It's worth reflecting on the changes of fortune. In 1970 Fiedler and Goodman were very big names, while Algren was a half-forgotten relic. Now, for nearly a decade, Algren has been an "in" writer. When a copy of *Growing Up Absurd* was found in Ted Kaczynski's cabin, it made me think of Goodman for the first time in years. Today Fiedler's name means about as much to readers under forty as that of John Jay Chapman, Karl Shapiro, or Orville Prescott.)

With one exception, I had encountered every name mentioned in the book. The exception, it turned out, was the subject of a chapter in itself: "I Talk To Alan Kapelner." The chapter was Krim's interview with the writer, dated 1967. The acknowledgments page did not list this chapter as having previously appeared in a magazine, as was the case with most of the book's contents. I can only presume that Krim intended to place the article with a magazine and was unable to do so. Nonetheless, it was clear, from the prefatory statements, that he regarded Kapelner as important:

"Both men [James Jones and Norman Mailer] along with Alan Kapelner of our mutual generation (and James T. Farrell of the older one) have by their almost unconscious behavior taught me root-truths about the boldness necessary for being an American writer of consequence. I have learned from everyone, but I hold these four special... Kapelner (too little known) is seasoned, unique, resourceful, beautifully cocky toward existence and humble to individuals he respects, a writer lying in wait for readers, practically undiscovered in the overpopulated wilderness of the U.S. 60s."

If one is familiar with the comparative rank accorded Jones, Mailer, and Farrell in 1970, one will realize that Krim was putting this Alan Kapelner in heavy company. Jones, though now remembered chiefly for having made it possible for Sinatra to win an Oscar, would then have appeared on many short-lists of the American writers most likely to win a Nobel. The same thing would have applied to Farrell, who had been a considerable influence on Mailer, Jones, and many other writers of the Depression and World War II generations. Mailer, of course, was the overwhelming favorite to win the Nobel, rather than Saul Bellow; Toni Morrison was some months away from publishing her first book when Krim was

writing his words.

Several things of interest emerged at once:

1. Krim clearly regarded Kapelner as a sort of precursor to the Beat Generation, or, at least, a fellow-traveler in the mold of Chandler Brossard. Kapelner did not so see himself, calmly dodging each opening Krim gave him in that area. He was not interested in belonging to a literary school.

2. Kapelner paraphrases Dan Wakefield, author of a number of well-reviewed novels in the Sixties and Seventies, as saying, "Gee, you did it so long ago, and now people are getting on that sort of thing without even knowing of [Kapelner's first novel] *Lonely Boy Blues*." Later on, I looked through Wakefield's memoirs of life in the Village in the Fifties and Sixties, published around 1989; Alan Kapelner's name does not appear. Nor does it appear in similar books by Samuel Delany, Ron Sukenick, the late Anatole Broyard, or any other chronicler of the period, except one other book of Krim's: his posthumous anthology, where Kapelner is mentioned once as having been a neighbor of Peter LaFarge's — a folksinger who was a close friend of Dylan's until his suicide. "That sort of thing," in the context of the interview, refers to Kapelner's book having been the prototype of a thousand subsequent chronicles of children caught in suffocating relationships with their parents — from Bruce Jay Friedman's *A Mother's Kisses* to Phillip Roth's *Portnoy's Complaint* to, moving further afield, *A Confederacy of Dunces*. None of these writers, though, show any familiarity with Kapelner's work.

3. Kapelner's aforementioned first novel had been published in 1944 by Scribners under the auspices of Maxwell Perkins, still by common consensus the greatest editor of literary fiction in American history, the man who molded Fitzgerald, Hemingway, and Thomas Wolfe into touchstones of the written word. Also, at one point in the interview Kapelner brushes aside a comparison Krim was making with Louis-Ferdinand Celine by saying, "Of course, being a Jew, I dislike Celine on other levels." Until reading this, I thought that Henry Roth, who started the follow-up to *Call It Sleep* under Perkins' supervision and then abandoned it, was the only Jewish-American novelist to work with Perkins — but this Kapelner had finished and published his book. It should be noted, however, that no major or minor characters in Kapelner's published work is identified as Jewish.

I resolved to look up the entries in *Book Review Digest* for Kapelner's two novels. The review-snippets I read were intriguing, to say the least. Concerning *Lonely Boy Blues*, I found:

Mr. Kapelner's effort to tell this in "the beat of

the blues" leads him into all sorts of strange mannerisms . . . . Despite the use of these devices, *Lonely Boy Blues* bears a strong resemblance to what used to be called proletarian novels.
— Herbert Kupferberg [Tuli's brother] in *Weekly Book Review*.

What Kupferberg meant by "strange mannerisms" was more fully explained in *Saturday Review*'s notice. There N. L. Rothman wrote that the book used verbal experimentation of the type last seen in transition, the quintessential "revolution of the word" journal, while dealing with themes reminiscent of Farrell and William Saroyan.

The excerpt of reviews of Kapelner's second novel and only other book, *All The Naked Heroes*, published by Braziller in 1960, were even more interesting. Maxwell Geismar, Nelson Algren's leading champion among the American critics of the period, had this to say in the *New York Herald Tribune* book section:

A novel of the 30s, acrid, angry, desperate — sometimes sentimental — but also full of a folk humor and folk wisdom that we have not had in our literature for quite a while. It is a kind of prose-poem of the decade more than a strict novel: a panorama of the period in the bitter brilliant tone of the early Dos Passos. It casts a hard and scornful light on the social criticism of such recent writers as Norman Mailer, and it makes the beatniks look like the disturbed and mystic children that they are. Perhaps the only real comparison with Mr. Kapelner's chronicle, and the only recent rival it has had, is Nelson Algren's *A Walk on the Wild Side*. . . . This novel indeed, coming so late in time as it does, forms a curious link between the "art novels" of the 20s and the "beat novels" of the 50s.

Other reviewers were not so enthusiastic. David Dempsey, in the *New York Times Book Review*, remarked: "This book appears to the reader as a sort of double-glazed plateglass window . . . . The experiment (if such it is) is not entirely successful. Mr. Kapelner's style has what is usually called 'vitality,' in this case, the vitality of a pneumatic drill tearing up Third Avenue." *Kirkus Reviews* called it "desperately earnest but pathetically inept," and asserted: "The most disturbing and unforgivable element in this first [sic] novel is the fact that although the setting is supposedly the thirties in America the situations and characters belong to the Beat Generation."

Though I have talked with a man who saw him as recently as 1990, Kapelner has published nothing since a short story appeared in 1970. The only photo of him I have seen, on the jacket of his second book, shows a man who appears to be in his early forties, with narrowed eyes and stern mouth who resembles nothing so much as a tanned, macho version of Steely Dan's Donald Fagen. An early volume of *Contemporary Authors* that carries an entry for Kapelner gives no birthdate or birthplace, stating: "Kapelner explains his missing personal data with these words: 'The work of a writer is enough for inclusion.'" But the 1955 anthology *New Voices 2* includes a contributor's note that is slightly more forthcoming. It states that Kapelner was "born in Brooklyn, where he attended P.S. 164 and Erasmus Hall High School, afterwards taking courses at the New School." A 1984 Manhattan phone book gives an address and phone number for an Alan Kapelner; there is no such listing in the current phone book. When I called the number I got a modem tone, and am inclined to think the number belongs to someone else.

It is plain from the variety of stylistic influences in *Lonely Boy Blues*, however, that Kapelner had read widely in modern American fiction before he started writing. Music was an even greater influence. The title *Lonely Boy Blues* is taken from a 1942 record by Jay McShann's Kansas City jazz band that featured one of Charlie Parker's earliest recorded solos, and Kapelner was quoted in his 1944 biographical writeup in the *New York Times Book Review*, as saying that he had written the book with jazz and boogie-woogie records playing nonstop, seeking to capture their rhythm in his text. It is remarkable how close Kapelner came, in some of this novel's passages, to devising his own version of "spontaneous bop prosody" nearly a decade before Kerouac wrote *On The Road*.

What is really startling is to find Maxwell Perkins, who steered Thomas Wolfe and Fitzgerald away from heavy experimentation, not only accepting a book like this but seeing it through the press in the fall of 1944, at a time when paper shortages were most pronounced and only the most surefire sellers were seeing print. The third paragraph of *Lonely Boy Blues* gives an idea of how starkly it contrasted with the Kathleen Winsor historical romances and Ernie Pyle war journalism of the day:

Now let's get this straight:
The flesh spins to the skull, and discharging in
the skull lives the brain, jackpot brain, passport

Metaphor to Action

Whether it is a speaker, taut on a platform,
who battles a crowd with the hammers of his words,
whether it is the crash of lips on lips
after absence and wanting : we must close
the circuits of ideas, now generate,
that leap in the body's action or the mind's repose.

Over us is a striking on the walls of the sky,
here are the dynamos, steel-black, harboring flame,
here is the man night-walking who derives
tomorrow's manifestoes from this midnight's meeting   ;
here we require the proof in solidarity,
iron on iron, body on body, and the large single beating.

And behind us in time are the men who second us
as we continue.   And near us is our love   :
no forced contempt, no refusal in dogma, the close
of the circuit in a fierce dazzle of purity.
And over us is night a field of pansies unfolding,
charging with heat its softness in a symbol
to weld and prepare for action our minds' intensity.

— Muriel Rukeyser

(From *Theory of Flight*, 1935. Reprinted with permission.)

to a future, mardi-gras destiny drowning in confetti and wine. The future belongs to you, you are the future. Very elementary, my dear brain. Paste yourself to the bandwagon. Be the spoke in the wheel, you bitter American Dream brain, brain most likely not to succeed as a spoke, brain not knowing where it's going, but it's going. Oh, it's a good brain as far as good brains go, but as far as good brains go it went.

The first chapter in the book is related in the first person by a protagonist whose name we learn later is Chesty Anderson. He is walking around Times Square, ruminating to himself about the bums, the food, and his own vitality in a manner that seems to be borrowed from John Fante's *Ask The Dust* — now renowned as the book that inspired Charles Bukowski, but at the time a novel that had gotten lost in the shuffle. Or Kapelner may have gone straight to Knut Hamsun, from whom Fante learned the approach. Either way, the protagonist spots a prostitute whom he christens Kathleen in his mind. But before he can do anything she picks up an old man and steps into a hotel. Chesty returns to his home in Brooklyn and falls asleep. In the second chapter, he dreams of being married to the phantom Kathleen, of killing her, and of witnessing her resurrection and return. Following this short Joycean fantasia the book is written more or less in the third person.

Chapters 3, 4, and 5 are told from the points of view of Chesty's sister Mabel, brothers Joe and Skinny, and father Harry, respectively. There is also a mother, whose name is never given. Chesty and Mabel are grown, but since there's a war on they still live at home. Joe seems to be just short of thirteen, and Skinny is a teenager. Mabel has a boyfriend in the service. Harry is working in a war plant. Chesty, whose physical prowess is stressed, is waiting to be drafted.

It soon becomes clear that the atmosphere of the Anderson home is not only physically stifling (the three brothers share one bed), but spiritually so. "Mrs. Anderson" (as she is called in most of the book) is obsessed with keeping Mabel out of "trouble" before her soldier beau, in whom the daughter has already lost interest, comes home. Harry Anderson is deeply suspicious of the intellect and deeply admires anything involving physical bravado. He treats the thin, sickly, introspective Skinny contemptuously, encourages Joe to swagger (one entertaining chapter features Joe harassing the owner of a pool hall) and tolerates Chesty's interest in reading because the boy is so damn big and strong that he's sure to be a success in the Army.

Besides reading, Chesty is also interested in writing; in Chapter 6, the narrative comes to a halt while he reads a 37-line poem to his uncomprehending friends. If *Lonely Boy Blues*

had come out fifteen years later, the poem would have been a perfect parody of high Beat coffeehouse fare, with clever Corsoesque echoes. But since it appears in a book published a few months before the Battle of the Bulge, it only makes sense as a pastiche of William Carlos Williams and Kenneth Patchen:

a yellow horn
ripped
    the smoky room
and
    the pale girls
studied
    the pale girls.

This was extremely unfashionable stuff in 1944, when Karl Shapiro and Robert Lowell were winning acclaim for bringing rhyme and meter back to poetry, and this may explain why Kapelner became a novelist rather than a poet — not that he made any special effort to accommodate literary fashions with this book or its successor.

Chesty's attitude toward the war wavers between revulsion at having to be a part of it and simple resignation to the fact that being in it is something that he has to do. In this respect, the book reflects the views of many intelligent Americans of the period, and goes some way toward explaining the attitudes that emerged, inchoate, during the war and subsequently found their articulation in Existentialist philosophy. Nonetheless, the family drama is what counts in this book. Mabel finds a job in Washington, moves there, and is soon involved in an affair with a married bureaucrat. Her mother, receiving no letters, goes down to spend a weekend with her, and promptly dies in her sleep while next to her daughter in bed. Waking up, Mabel expresses not sorrow but only anger at the way her mother's demise is interfering with her liaison.

Meanwhile, Chesty is finally called up. He frets, gets drunk, gives the frail Skinny a pep talk, and goes to Manhattan for induction. But Chesty's physique proves a fraud; he has a heart murmur and is classified 4-F. He goes home and breaks the news to his father. The old man, it turns out, has just received a beating from some strangers in a bar, shattering his own notions of being a strongman. Hearing this news, Harry goes into a reverie where the whole story of his life flashes before his eyes. Kapelner thus makes rather obviously the point he summarizes when talking about the novel to Seymour Krim: the book is about "the failed men and women, greedy, hungering to resurrect themselves in their children. To relive their lives in their children, never realizing they're destroying their children." Harry Anderson drives it home by attacking his 4-F son, heart murmur and all. The last paragraph of the novel does not make it clear whether Chesty is actually dying of shock at the assault, but is worth quoting in its entirety:

> But the helpless terror and the bewildered terror smothered the cry, and he looked at his brothers and their eyes were open to witness his terror and the old man's fists, and he saw the tears in Skinny's eyes, and he wanted to hold him very close and tell him how he felt so very close to him, and he looked at Joe and Joe was grinning and glowing, and he looked up at the old man and saw the face of an old beast, and he was captured by some hungry appetite to inspect the livid welts that coughed from his body and face, but the drive of the saturating fists strained his senses, and he collapsed into an endless pit of exhaustion, and the room became a frenzied whirlpool, and he was being sucked into the whirlpool, and everything went around and down like a ball rolling around and down and down a hill, down, down, around and down, the ball rolled and rolled down, down, around and down, and down the hill, and the pain in his body stopped screaming, and the canopy of the soaking blows that came like the precise rhythm of a fugue were incapable of penetrating the blankness, the catacombs of his mind. No, not anymore.

It's obvious why Perkins was willing to fight wartime shortages to get the book published. Kapelner is employing Steinian repetition and Joycean onomatopoeia with no small skill here, and with far greater control, stylistically speaking, than he would in his second novel. The double meaning of "fugue" — Chesty may or may not be in just that psychiatric state — is utilized superbly. There are several other passages in the book that are nearly as well-done.

Kapelner's more obvious verbal pyrotechnics — lines from nearly a hundred popular songs are woven through a book that runs 127 pages in its paperback edition, none of which are encumbered with quotation marks — conceal the full extent to which he echoes earlier books. It was not until I transcribed the above paragraph, for instance, that I realized that the three Anderson brothers are patterned after the Brothers Karamazov.

Lonely Boy Blues was the most thoroughgoingly experimental book edited by Max Perkins (mysteriously, Kapelner is not mentioned in A. Scott Berg's otherwise definitive biography of the editor). It was a fine beginning for a writer still in his early twenties. Anthony Quinn later purchased the motion picture rights to the novel, and in 1956 it was issued in paperback by Jim Bryans at Lion Books (which issued most of Jim Thompson's best books). But it never generated much in the way of sales. "After *Blues*," Kapelner told Krim, "I didn't know what to do with my time. I screwed around a lot, I wasted a lot of years . . . . I first came down to the Village then, I didn't know what life was like, I wanted to see paintings."

He goes on to say that his second novel, *All The Naked Heroes*, was initially called *Strangers In The Midnight World*. "And a lot of publishers told me to put it away. It was during the McCarthy period. Random House . . . Little Brown put it away. I got a lot of letters, and always specifically, 'This is not the time for a book of this kind.' . . . So I read the book . . . and I said it's a lousy book. I thought I'd write this entire book over again from beginning to end . . . And I got used to a sense of language which never occurred to me before. Certain sounds of words, rhythms, feelings for words. It could be one of the debits of *All The Naked Heroes*, the romance with words."

While Kapelner's first book echoed The Brothers Karamazov, *All the Naked Heroes* nearly echoes the Gilgamesh epic, and has a similarly elemental feel. Ripley (Rip for short) and Paul Gomery are brothers in Manhattan. It begins, quite specifically, on August 12, 1938. The Munich Crisis is weeks away and war talk is in the air. Rip is disturbed by the prospect of the oncoming war. Paul is more than disturbed; he can think of nothing else. Four days before, their mother Anita has died, leaving a letter to them and their father, Steve:

> Due to the fact that you, my husband, Steven Gomery, consciously brought me cruelties and cruelties during the last five sick years of my life, I, your wife, Anita Gomery, sane in mind, leave to you the sum of $2 on the following conditions: that you use $1 of the sum to buy yourself a last meal, and the remaining $1 to buy a rope to hang yourself. To my sons, Paul and Ripley, I, Anita Gomery, leave the total sum of my savings, $697. May they live a kind, kind, kind life.

The father promptly disappears, and the brothers live for a while on the money (Paul has a job at a department store then gets himself fired) until it runs out. At this point, it becomes clear that Anita's last will and testament is more than merely a flip sendoff for the book's plot. The war and those responsible for creating it — Hitler, the Japanese militarists already slaughtering in China, the arms dealers and financiers who think a little conflict now and then a fine thing — are the threats to Rip and Paul's future. By vanishing, their father simultaneously fails to protect them against these predators, and joins the predators, a bit like Chesty Anderson's father did at the end of Kapelner's first book. Their mother leaves them with, essentially, the new Testament injunction to "resist ye not evil," so beloved of Tolstoy. The story of the book is how one brother resists not evil (less because of Christian charity than because of simple despair) and the other brother decides, finally, that engagement is preferable to distance.

At first it looks like Paul may have the better prospect of surviving, thanks to an episode that shows that Kapelner is not aiming for plausibility to make his point. Scanning a newspaper, Paul sees an ad asking one Billy Hathaway or anyone knowing his whereabouts to call Mary Hathaway. (The use of the maiden name of Shakespeare's wife is probably intentional, given what happens later.) He phones. It turns out that Mary is a woman his own age, and Billy is her missing younger brother. When he tells her he just wants to talk, she hangs up. He calls again, and launches into a "sensitive" speech which causes her to agree to a date. Not too plausible, of course, but as it turns out she has to be brought into the story, so Paul can embark on a love affair and the brothers can have something to fight about and part ways over.

Before too long the paths of the brothers have diverged. Paul falls in with a marijuana dealer and his circle of hopheads and becomes the kept man of a wealthy hausfrau. After he recovers his self-respect she ditches him. Before long he is on skid row, his journey to a final gin-sodden jump into the Hudson interrupted only when, in a highly effective chapter, he spots his father on the street, trails him to a hotel, then, without the nerve to directly confront him, calls the old man from a phone booth and alternately tries and refuses to establish communication despite what is either a bad connection or his father's refusal to admit the caller is known to him, or both.

Meanwhile, Rip decides to see America the boxcar way in the days before the onset of war. The scenes described in his journey range from acid in the manner of early Nelson Algren, to whimsical in the style of Saroyan, to a mixture of both, as in a scene where a "mouse-bodied girl" offers to cut off one of her ears and sell it to him.

The single most obvious stylistic hallmark of *All The Naked Heroes* is the constant use of nouns as verbs, in a style less grating on the ear than the early press conferences of Alexander Haig during his brief tenure as Secretary of State, but nonetheless obtrusive, and generally employed in an alliterative fashion that may or may not derive from Old Norse or Anglo-Saxon epics. "Bare-breasted girls beefed on the block," for instance. Or a turkey being "ovened," or potatoes "brown-sugared." Or men who "wolf-job" baked beans. Two or three similar examples may be found on almost every page (This mannerism also appears,

much less frequently, in *Lonely Boy Blues*) :

> [Rip] huckstered Eskimo Pies in a Bristol burlesque for room-money. Top banana: Bango Yancey, deathcell'd in a nightmare of unclimbed ladders to fame. Strip queen. Juicy 'Love Me' Janel, camouflaged lesbian, hater of her birth and body and thirty years of busty fruits. Watched Bango and 'Love Me' feed raw jokes and breasts and belly to a fever-glutted audience. Saw eyes fry and blur and breaths hiss and lips puff and legs wag and hands race into pockets. Smelled the smell of wet conquests.

The apostrophe on "deathcell'd" tips the reader off to what Kapelner is really up to here. Rip's saga is really a late-depression version of Walt Whitman's Specimen Days. And it comes as no surprise that this process of "finding" America is dispositive in making Rip's destiny different from Paul's.

Paul, in Manhattan, falls into what was then the tight subculture of pot smokers. (It is doubtful that any but the hippest critics noted that Kapelner employed drug slang of a mid-to-late Forties vintage in these chapters, rather than terms common when he was writing. The interesting thing is that the context in which it is used is not quite the same as it was within the gay culture of the 1950s where Susan Sontag picked it up from Alfred Chester. Kapelner's pot smokers use "campy" as a general term of approval, with just an echo of the later meaning of the word, that something is a compound of cute, quaint, and *outré*.) After failing to adjust to that culture, he falls out of it and into the less demanding circle of Bowery bums. But even there he cannot handle the minimal terms of survival. His world, in other words, shrinks from Manhattan to lower Manhattan to the Bowery to the bottom of the river. Rip, by contrast, expands his horizons from Manhattan to cover all America.

Both brothers, at the start of the book, have aspirations to be writers; Rip to articulate a sense of wonder at life tempered with awareness of its dark side, Paul to articulate his rage at its dark side. The only writing that Paul can do, by book's end, is to send his draft card back to FDR with a letter that demonstrates why Kapelner could find no publisher in the early Fifties, and why nearly any other publisher besides George Braziller might have balked at the book's theme at the high point of the Cold War:

> These tragedy makers should, by law, be so sacredly entitled to the deathliness they manufactured. They, these sick plaguing sick, are Hitler's makers. They plucked him from hell to murder a German Republic. They babied him, they nursed him and coddled him and fed him and fattened him and schooled him and uniformed him. They electrified him with a

Party and an Army, and the makers' creature murdered the Republic. But as it comes to all dark makers, creatures betray the minds that create them, and Adolf Hitler knifed his bonds and plundered his makers' trade and international loot and conquered their lands and today crazes to bleed and boss their world.

In other words, Paul would not be surprised to read the current articles regarding the activities of the Bank of International Settlements involving assets looted by the Nazis from their victims. But after writing this letter, Paul has a change of heart, hurries back to the mailbox into which he has dropped it, and persuades the postman to give it back to him.

Rip continues to resolve to be a writer, providing he survives the war (for he has decided, unlike Paul, to come to grips with the world). Even so his intention is not to achieve fame. Kapelner thought highly enough of what he has Rip write to Mary that he repeated the words from the book, slightly revised, in his *Contemporary Authors* entry:

> ... what a rough tough lonely job serious writers have. To make points, to make ideas stick in hope of re-routing minds ... they've got to just about rape people with words ... It seems to me too many writers write as if they were committing acts of espionage. When reading their work, it always seems they've spied on and stolen some great writer's state secrets. [In *CA* a few years later, Kapelner changed the passage to read, "He should steal *no man's* state secrets."] I think a writer should be enslaved to no dead or living god. He should create strictly from his own personality. His signature should be so deeply his own.

This goes some way toward explaining why Kapelner published so little and why he was disinclined to push his work on the public in the fashion of other writers.

It should finally be said about this second novel that, as Maxwell Geismar noted, it has something in common with the more lyrical side of Thirties fiction, from Dos Passos to Henry Roth to John Fante. At the the same time much of it reflects the acid, sardonic side of that same decade, from Nathanael West to Daniel Fuchs' *Low Company*. But what is especially striking to a reader in 1997 is the extent which the novel presages the fantastic, verbally extravagant fiction that emerged later in the Sixties and whose vogue lasted long enough into the Seventies that Jerome Klinkowitz, Thomas LeClair and Larry McCaffrey were able to write whole books about it. I refer to such "postmodern" works as Ron Sukenick's *Up and Out*, Steve Katz's *The Exaggerations of Peter Prince* and *Creamy and Delicious*, the novels of Raymond Federman and Jonathan Baumbach, Frederick Barthelme's earliest work, and other such examples of what was termed "metafiction." None of these writers, in books or interviews, refers to Kapelner however, making him quite an anomaly in literary history.

Kapelner's entry for *Contemporary Authors*, probably written in 1963, indicates that he was writing a "contemporary novel on boredom" for Braziller. There is no telling if this is the same book that he discusses in the 1967 interview with Seymour Krim. There Kapelner calls the book *The Air-Conditioned Hell*, and states that he has just rewritten it, as he did his previous book: "I first wrote it in first person and it satisfied me." In a footnote, written three years later, Krim states: "As this collection goes to press, Kapelner is rewriting his book yet a third time." The novel never appeared.

Last year I was taking down three copies of *All The Naked Heroes* from a shelf at the Strand Book Store in Manhattan when a man exclaimed from the foot of the ladder: "What are you doing with those books by Alan Kapelner?" The man turned out to be a fairly well-known author of latter-day metafiction who had not only read Kapelner's books but had met him at a writer's colony in Virginia in 1988 and had stopped by to see him in Manhattan once or twice over the following two years. This writer told me that Kapelner, at the colony, spoke little about whatever he was working on, but talked a bit about his past work, and told a couple of stories about his sessions with Max Perkins, which startled a good many of the younger listeners. Kapelner also told him that he had taught on occasion at Hofstra University. But he had heard nothing about Kapelner in six years.

And that, as things stand, is the story of an author whose idiosyncratic and experimental novels, scouring disparate styles and decades in a serious attempt to make sense of the journey this nation took over thirty years, occupy a literary place all by themselves.

Confessions of a Labor Editor

Jim McNeill

I THINK it was sometime in December 1993, only nine months after arriving in Racine, Wisconsin, that I began to lose it. I'd always been a slow writer, and the weekly deadlines at *Racine Labor* were beginning to beat me down. Of course, working for a union paper, I'd been drinking. Soon after Thanksgiving I began to feel an odd twitch in my right side. "Liver pains," a friend at the Racine Labor Center bar suspected. "And you're only twenty-nine. Impressive."

During solitary lunches at the local KFC, I began muttering to myself while scanning the *Wall Street Journal* — required reading since it's the only daily paper in America that still takes labor seriously. Then one day a particularly noxious Paul Gigot column sent me straight over the edge. I did the one thing that every journalist knows to be a clear sign of dementia. I dashed off an outraged letter to the editor. I regretted it as soon as I sent it. But in my addled state — driven by deadlines, numbed by alcohol — the whole ugly episode was quickly forgotten.

And then, on the morning of December 30th — the day *Racine Labor*'s special year-end issue was supposed to go to press (it didn't) — I got a very strange long distance call.

"I just wanted to thank you. I can't give you my name, but I wanted you to know that there are many people here who really appreciate what you said."

"Excuse me?"

"What you said, what you wrote."

"What?"

"In the *Wall Street Journal*."

And there it was. The lead letter in the December 30th issue. They'd entitled my missive, "Fewer Smokestacks, More Poverty." Not exactly my point, but not entirely inaccurate either. Gigot had praised Wisconsin Gov. Tommy Thompson for bravely reforming Wisconsin's welfare system and creating thousands of new jobs. I argued that Thompson's welfare pilot programs had failed, and that meanwhile he had deliberately allowed high-paying, unionized factory jobs to disappear, turning Wisconsin into a low-wage haven for business.

In the coming days, I would receive responses even stranger than the first. In mid-January, I received a thick parcel from the Interhemispheric Bering Strait Tunnel & Railroad Group, a Moscow-based outfit intent on building a 4,500-mile rail link between Russia and the United States. "Reading in *Wall Street Journal* your article on Smoke Stack America I feel that this letter will get into right hands," the cover letter began. It went on to explain that, yes, the project would despoil huge swaths of untrammeled wilderness in Alaska and Siberia. But it would create tens of thousands of union jobs! Sounded good to me.

Given the fact that I had started out as nothing less than an environmental reporter at *In These Times*, the left-liberal newsmagazine in Chicago, the packet made for one of those little ironies with which a journalist's

For three days running in September 1995 a hundred quarter dollar coins were firmly super-glued on Wall Street in

career is littered.

Another was the timing of my decision to hitch my star to the labor movement. In 1993, when I started at *Racine Labor*, a catatonic Lane Kirkland still occupied the eighth floor of the AFL-CIO's headquarters and to most the American labor movement seemed little more than a decaying corpse. This was long before John Sweeney's insurgents would topple labor's *ancien régime*, and years before fresh-faced college students would clamor to join the AFL-CIO's Union Summer. Back then, only the stray historian — equipped with a coroner's stomach and a eulogist's pen — even bothered to examine labor's putrefying flesh.

I wish I could claim that I went to Racine like some latter-day Dos Passos character, selflessly committed to the cause of the "worker." Unfortunately, the truth is far less heroic. In late 1992, I was downsized by the eternally insolvent *In These Times*. When *Racine Labor* called the next spring, I was ready to relocate.

Huddled along Lake Michigan 70 miles north of Chicago, Racine is a prototypical Rust Belt town of 85,000. With its crumbling brick factories and struggling downtown, Racine is the land that post-industrial America is trying hard to forget. Not all of its factories have closed, and in many of them union workers still bargain collectively with management for fair wages. It's an economic arrangement as outmoded — and dangerous — as the New Deal legislation that makes it possible.

Even worse, people in old union towns like Racine still cling to archaic ideas like economic democracy. With their demands for fair wages and decent benefits, they set a very bad example for a population supposed to be awed by the power of the global economy. The mulish persistence of union workers in cities like Racine provides an unsettling reminder that only three decades ago, the American labor movement regularly mounted more strikes than any other union movement on earth.

A STRIKE broke out during my first month in Racine. Like so many great labor battles, this one involved automobiles — GM automobiles. Of course, this was Racine in 1993 — not Flint in '37 — so the walkout wasn't aimed at a crucial parts plant. This strike involved just 33 Teamsters in the service department of a local Oldsmobile dealer. Nevertheless, it featured all the drama — and tragedy — that accompany much larger strikes.

Life on the picket line at Frank Gentile Oldsmobile had been fun at first. For two weeks, the strikers had wandered up and down Highway 20, enjoying the mercifully warm Wisconsin spring, waving righteously at the union faithful who honked as they went by. The Gentile pickets even had fun flipping off scabs as they drove into the dealer's lot. But then, while a dozen Teamsters meandered slowly past the side entrance, a scab gunned his car through the picket line, plowing a striker up on the hood and depositing him back on the pavement.

The striker, bruised but not badly hurt, was still screaming about it when I showed up with my notebook. "These people are willing to kill you. Literally fucking kill you!" Of course, the company didn't *really* want to kill him.

different places — on the road, on sidewalks and on subway staircases. They found an inseparable connection. The

Gentile was happy to just permanently replace him instead.

Like so many unionized firms, Gentile seemed to relish the prospect of a walkout. In the negotiations leading up to the strike, the Olds dealer called in Wisconsin's premier union-busting law firm to bargain with the Teamsters. The union asked for a modest raise in its hourly wage. Gentile's attorneys countered by saying they were going to wipe out the hourly wage altogether and replace it with a piece-work pay scheme. With some workers likely to lose as much as $10,000 a year, the Teamsters decided they had to strike.

It's a decision that very few unions are still willing to make. In 1977, there were 3,111 work stoppages in the United States. In 1981, however, Ronald Reagan famously replaced the nation's striking air traffic controllers and wiped out their union. Companies across the country quickly followed Reagan's lead, seeing every strike as an opportunity to destroy their unions. By 1996, the number of walkouts was down to 372. As the Gentile strike entered its second month, and the company showed no signs of settling, I began to understand why unions stopped striking.

U NIONS in Racine have always been more militant than most. In 1933, Racine was one of the first cities to be swept up in the wave of organizing triggered by the passage of the National Industrial Recovery Act. Racine gained notoriety as America's "Little Moscow" as the city's socialist-led labor council organized dozens of local factories. In March 1934, when a strike in Racine paralyzed the Nash auto plant — and shuttered the company's main

quarter dollars resisted the bankers and brokers clutches and did not become a part of daily Wall Street money

factory in Kenosha as well — President Roosevelt summoned the leader of the Racine local to the White House. He returned from Washington with the assurance that FDR had taken "a personal interest" in the strike. Less than a month later, the company settled, and soon Nash's Racine employees were helping produce the first union-made cars in America. This was three years before the UAW's famous sit-down strike against GM in Flint and seven years before the union would initial its first contract with Ford.

Since 1896, when striking typographers in Racine started their own daily newspaper, the city's labor battles have been recorded, and urged along, by a series of left-leaning union papers. *Racine Labor* was founded in 1941, when the city's unions hired a socialist from the Illinois coal fields, Loren Norman, to edit it. For 30 years, most of them during the red-crazed days of the Cold War, Norman published a remarkably progressive paper. He condemned the witch hunts of Wisconsin Sen. Joseph McCarthy, was an early opponent of the Vietnam War, and in 1968 supported Eugene McCarthy's anti-war crusade for president. Norman even published front-page pictures of long-haired youths getting "clean for Gene." In 1972, Norman was succeeded as editor by Richard Olson, a U.S. Army veteran who'd protested the war while still in the service. Olson came to *Racine Labor* after leading an organizing drive in a Wisconsin cannery, and left in 1979 to join the UAW's national staff. Olson's successor, and my immediate predecessor, was Roger Bybee, a Racine native who'd long been a mainstay in southeastern Wisconsin's progressive political community.

I was hardly qualified to carry on their tradition. I grew up conservative in upstate New York, the dutiful son of a General Electric middle manager. My earliest exposure to labor came through my father's laments against his plant's militant union president. Though proselytized by leftists in college, I learned little about labor during my conversion experience. Unions once had influence on campus — the UAW gave crucial support to Students for a Democratic Society in the early Sixties — but labor was anything but hip when I reached college in the Eighties. I finally picked up a few facts about unions at *In These Times*, but I arrived in Racine remarkably naive about how the labor movement actually worked. The strike at Gentile Oldsmobile, small as it was, would open my eyes.

I had assumed, since there were only 33 Teamsters working at Gentile, that the strike, even if it went badly, wouldn't have repercussions far beyond the dealer's lot. It turned out, however, that the Teamsters didn't just represent the Gentile workers, they also represented nearly 200 employees in the half dozen other car dealerships in town. Over the years, the Teamsters had bargained with all the dealerships in Racine to create a roughly equivalent wage and benefit pattern at all the dealerships. The brilliance of this kind of pattern bargaining is that it stops competing companies from trying to undercut one another by paying lower wages to their employees. Pattern bargaining means that workers are no longer pawns in an industry's war. Of course, when one company breaks the pattern — as Gentile was trying to do — the system collapses.

I was beginning to perceive, in microcosm, the magnitude of the troubles that faced the American labor movement. Before leaving Chicago, I'd dutifully read *Which Side Are You On?*, Thomas Geoghegan's impossibly bleak book about his life as a labor lawyer during the Seventies and Eighties. But I'd assumed that its darkest passages reflected some sort of Irish-Catholic inner turmoil, not the actual state of American unions. But as I would discover, Geoghegan had, if anything, soft-pedaled labor's problems.

Look at Racine. In the late Seventies, *Racine Labor* had roughly 15,000 subscribers, virtually all of them union members making good money in stable jobs. By 1993, *Racine Labor* had barely 7,000 subscribers. It's hard to exaggerate the economic devastation wrought by the loss of those union jobs. On average, union members make 33 percent more than non-union workers. Once cast out of Eden, they trudge into the non-union world, lucky to make $7 an hour extruding children's toys. And America's bizarrely stacked labor laws make it increasingly difficult to bring unorganized workers back into the union fold.

In 1993, the fall of union power in this corner of Wisconsin was nowhere more apparent than at the Racine Labor Center. Sitting in a sea of tarmac, with sickly shrubs guarding the entrance, the Labor Center was virtually devoid of vegetation but awash in red ink. Built in the Fifties by the city's CIO unions, the Labor Center still boasted a 400-person meeting hall, plenty of office space and a well-stocked bar. But now Bingo fund-raisers filled the main hall more often than union conclaves, and many of the offices

transactions. Photographs were taken as people attempted to pick up the quarters. Several days later these photographs were

were empty since the unions that once inhabited them had ceased to exist.

Thankfully, the Labor Center bar was open almost every night. Profoundly depressed by the antics of the non-union youth at Racine's "Vintage Rock Cafe," I preferred the company of the Labor Center's UAW retirees. Over shots of Hot Damn, the retirees — along with the occasional active member — would relate to me the fine points of labor politics, with the strike at Gentile offered as an increasingly ominous object lesson. As the strike lingered into its third month, a leader of one small UAW local, which had been on strike several years before, wondered "what the hell was wrong" with the Teamsters.

"They've gotta start getting serious."

What should they do?

"They've gotta focus on three things: Solidarity, sabotage, and vandalism." (Hmm....) These were the indispensable ingredients of any successful strike, he said. I had heard stories that, during his strike, manure had been dumped down the skylights of the plant and onto the machines. I asked him if the stories were true. He just winked and bought me a beer.

Ironically, even as the Teamsters at Gentile languished out on Highway 20, no union seemed more militant on the national level in 1993 than the "New Teamsters." Led by Ron Carey, the reformer who'd won the presidency in the union's first-ever rank-and-file election in 1991, the Teamsters bargained hard with United Parcel Service and later successfully struck the nation's major trucking companies.

But Bert Thomas, the head of the Racine local, was no "New Teamster." When Thomas bothered to come to the Gentile picket line, he always showed up in a late-model American luxury car. One day Thomas promised to give a striker $10 if he'd burn his New Teamsters hat. As the strike dragged on, the rift between Thomas and the rank and file grew.

Gentile, of course, claimed that the service department payroll had been killing its business. And, of course, the Teamsters replied, how then had the company survived three months of dismal sales caused by the strike? But winning such arguments counts little in the field of industrial combat, and while Gentile refused to bend, the workers were beginning to break. None of the Teamsters had crossed the picket line, but by the fourth month many had given up on both Gentile and the union, and found other work.

Back at the Labor Center, talk about the Teamsters — and Thomas particularly — grew more heated. (Of course, none of this went into the labor paper.) Clearly, the strike was entering a crisis phase, but Thomas didn't seem to have a strategy for keeping the members involved or rallying outside support. This was especially inexcusable given the union heroics of Racine's past.

D ICK FOUGHT, who ran the Labor Center when I arrived in Racine, was a legendary character who liked to rail against the spineless "bootlickers" and comfortable "fat cats" (the union hierarchies and staff) who were destroying the movement. Dick had earned the right to complain: During the troubled Eighties he had been president of the union at Racine Steel, and he had managed to keep both his local and the company alive during a series of vicious corporate attacks. In 1980, corporate

exhibited on the same street where the quarters had been placed. – p.t.t.red

raider Victor Posner purchased Racine Steel and, as with his other acquisitions, quickly proceeded to bleed it dry. In 1983, as Posner's vast holdings lost $45 million, he took $10.4 million in salary and bonuses. In 1985, the year Racine Steel was taken through bankruptcy, Posner garnered $12.7 million, making him the highest-paid CEO in the United States.

A bankruptcy judge eventually unloaded Racine Steel on a local partnership led by a 31-year-old securities dealer who had previously been censured for selling bogus investments to retirees. When the new owners insisted that the company could survive only in a "union-free" environment, Dick and the local started pressuring Racine's City Council to cancel a bond issue vital to the company. The partners quickly returned to the bargaining table. When they then demanded that the union accept pay cuts of roughly $2 an hour, Dick sought strike authorization from the membership: they gave it to him in a 249-to-8 vote. Again, the partners relented. Eventually, the union members accepted a contract with modest pay cuts, but with strengthened grievance procedures. In an era of plant-closings and de-certs, it was a remarkable victory.

But that wasn't how things were playing out at Gentile. As the strike ground into its fifth month, the picket line turned ugly. On the increasingly rare occasions when Thomas showed up at the dealership, the workers barely acknowledged his presence. When Thomas finally scheduled a community-wide rally in front of Gentile, the strikers organized a separate demonstration of their own. It was a very bad sign.

Finally, the two

sides reached an agreement near the end of the strike's fifth month. The union was permitted to stay, but under a "modified" piece-work pay scale. The scabs, naturally, kept their new jobs. Most of the original Teamsters were long gone. Some of the younger guys seemed to have just disappeared. With the older members, I heard rumors of broken marriages and repossessed cars, but it wasn't something the Teamsters wanted pursued in *Racine Labor*. Reporting on the settlement, I called it a draw. Perhaps, given the state of American labor law, it was.

Three months later I had my run-in with the *Wall Street Journal*. In early 1994, just as the twitch in my side graduated to a throb, a temporarily flush *In These Times* called and asked me to return. By April, I was back in Chicago.

I've been back to Racine, of course, lured by the Labor Center's cheap drafts and priceless conversation. There's been no magic transformation since I left, but the new leadership at the AFL-CIO has clearly convinced many people that labor is entering an historic era of rebirth. John Sweeney may not be the reincarnation of John L. Lewis, but he has reopened debates within the labor movement that have been closed since the Thirties. And while Sweeney has yet to score any great victories, consider how feeble even the great organizing drives of the Thirties looked at times. By 1939, after a severe economic downturn and bitter union in-fighting, the UAW's dues-paying membership at GM had dropped to only 6 percent of the workforce. Many CIO unions were in the same beleaguered state. Only the arrival of the World War II boom ensured that the new unions would survive.

Even more to the point, in company towns like Flint, corporations controlled public culture more effectively then than they do now. By the Thirties, the fierce "Americanism" campaigns of World War I and the Twenties had assimilated most of the nation's vast immigrant population into the culture of laissez-faire capitalism. But, as historian Gary Gerstle argues in *Working-Class Americanism*, those hyper-patriotic campaigns unintentionally created expectations among white ethnics that they would be fully included in the democratic and material promise of American life. When the moribund capitalism of the Depression failed to deliver on that promise, those newly emboldened Americans looked to the labor movement for relief. Today, our advertisers peddle an even more potent brand of Americanism, a hyper-consumerism that promises personal liberation on a scale never before imagined. But once again, American capitalism is having trouble delivering the goods. Twenty years of wage stagnation and record levels of income inequality have left many wondering how liberated they really are. Again,

many Americans are looking elsewhere for more authentic forms of liberation.

To exploit this opportunity labor must renew its efforts on what Michael Denning calls the "cultural front." Subsidizing a thousand new *Racine Labors* would be a start, but television is the medium that matters to a working-class audience. Since unions will never get more than token coverage on corporate TV, labor needs to start a cable network — and not a bland, PBS-style enterprise, either. Labor should hire a thousand Michael Moores and turn them loose producing sitcoms, documentaries and feature films. The idea is not without precedent. In 1926, the Chicago Federation of Labor launched WCFL, a broadly popular radio station that broadcast dramas, comedies, baseball games and decidedly anti-corporate news. At its peak, more than 100,000 households subscribed to WCFL's listener magazine. Perhaps, if we do it right, we can begin to create a society whose core values are rooted not in the privatized excess of the corporation but in the shared prosperity and collective purpose of the labor union.